MW00364303

1,001 PEARLS OF
SPIRITUAL WISDOM

1,001 PEARLS OF SPIRITUAL WISDOM

EDITED BY KIM LIM

Skyhorse Publishing

Skyhorse Publishing books may be purchased in bulk at special discounts for sales promotion, corporate gifts, fund-raising, or educational purposes. Special editions can also be created to specifications. For details, contact the Special Sales Department, Skyhorse Publishing, 307 West 36th Street, 11th Floor, New York, NY 10018 or info@skyhorsepublishing.com.

Skyhorse® and Skyhorse Publishing® are registered trademarks of Skyhorse Publishing, Inc.®, a Delaware corporation.

www.skyhorsepublishing.com

10 9 8 7 6 5 4 3 2 1

Library of Congress Cataloging-in-Publication Data is available on file.

ISBN: 978-1-62873-624-3

Printed in China

Contents

INTRODUCTION

Ironically, to begin an introduction to a quote book on spirituality, I am tempted to use a quote.

The reason is simple—spiritual things are beyond the body, and therefore beyond the grasp of language, which comes from the body. And yet, mankind has attempted throughout history to tie the soaring spirit down with words. We struggle to contain it within the confines of language, we dance with it in song, we force it into novels, wrestle it into poetry, and posit it in essays. As I gathered quotes for this book, I noticed that when fewer words were used to express the spirit, its meaning became more poignant. This makes sense. After all, how much more effective is a three-hundred page novel compared to a single line of poetry if both come to the same, inevitable conclusion that the spirit will always escape language? Perhaps the quote is the best medium to communicate spiritual wisdoms, epiphanies, and experiences.

It is astonishing to see the spectrum of people who supply the spiritual wisdoms in this little book. Not even half of the quotes here are attributed to religious leaders. I have quoted from eminent physicists, Hollywood heartthrobs, science-fiction authors, disgruntled philosophers, hard rockers, converted sportsmen, martyred politicians, hit TV shows, and church signboards. I quote from antiquity to modern day, from the Dalai Lama to Jesus Christ, from Sappho to Lauryn Hill. In our contemporary enlightened mindset, where science is regarded as incompatible with spirituality, we often forget that spirituality cannot be restricted to black and whites or human decision. The spirit exists in the infinite form of a god, in a blade of grass, in the geometry of equations, within oneself, and even, or perhaps especially, among a people. To deny spirituality as wishful thinking is to forget centuries of human engagement with the world, knowledge, art, love, the self, and the community. Even if you do not believe in the spiritual being, the involuntary human capacity to doubt is revealing in itself.

Some dismiss spiritual fancy as the unnecessary, even unethical, submission of the self to a greater power. Which begs the question: why should we be afraid of throwing ourselves headlong into mystery? As Graham Greene said, it is like falling in love; and who wouldn't want to be in love?

Kim Lim

TO BEGIN

"One must go further, one must go further."
This impulse to go further is an ancient thing in
the world.

—Søren Kierkegaard

We have the hunger for eternity in our souls, the
thought of eternity in our hearts, the destination for
eternity written on our inmost being.

—Alexander Maclaren

"What makes the desert beautiful," said the little
prince, "is that somewhere it hides a well . . ."

—Antoine de Saint-Exupéry, *The Little Prince*

The root of "spirit" is the Latin spirare, to breathe. Whatever lives on the breath, then, must have its spiritual dimension.

—Jane Hirshfield

It was the movement of the air that provided the image of spirituality, since the spirit borrows its name from the breath of wind…

—Sigmund Freud

The human soul is like a bird that is born in a cage. Nothing can deprive it of its natural longings, or obliterate the mysterious remembrance of its heritage.

—Epes Sargent

I believe the universe created us—we are an audience for miracles.

—Ray Bradbury

It's a basic fact about being human that sometimes the self seems to just melt away.

—Jonathan Haidt

The created world is but a small parenthesis in eternity.

—Thomas Browne

In the beginning was the myth. God, in his search for self-expression, invested the souls of Hindus, Greeks, and Germans with poetic shapes and continues to invest each child's soul with poetry every day.

—Herman Hesse

We are all writing God's poem.

—Anne Sexton

I think the real miracle is not to walk either on water or in thin air, but to walk on earth.

—Thích Nhất Hạnh

I've caught belief like a disease. I've fallen into belief like I fell in love.

—Graham Greene

I believe in Christianity as I believe that the sun has risen: not only because I see it, but because by it I see everything else.

—C. S. Lewis

I believe in everything until it's disproved. So I believe in fairies, the myths, dragons. . . . Who's to say that dreams and nightmares aren't as real as the here and now?

—John Lennon

God does not die on the day when we cease to
believe in a personal deity, but we die on the day
when our lives cease to be illumined by the steady
radiance, renewed daily, of a wonder, the source of
which is beyond all reason.

—Dag Hammarskjöld

A life is either all spiritual or not spiritual at all. No
man can serve two masters.

—Thomas Merton

Great men are they who see that spiritual is
stronger than any material force—that thoughts rule
the world.

—Ralph Waldo Emerson

Spirituality is a domain of awareness.

—Deepak Chopra

We don't have to change what we see. Only the way we see.

—Ann Voskamp

The only true voyage of discovery, the only fountain of Eternal Youth, would be not to visit strange lands but to possess other eyes...

—Marcel Proust

A spiritual man is happy with the whole existence. He says "yes" to the whole existence.

—Swami Dhyan Giten

TO BEGIN

We can no more do without spirituality than we can do without food, shelter, or clothing.

—Ernest Holmes

People know they are lacking something, they are constantly wanting some kind of spiritual guidance.

—Douglas Hurd

There is nothing besides a spiritual world...

—Franz Kafka

13

Rivers, ponds, lakes and streams—they all have
different names, but they all contain water. Just as
religions do—they all contain truths.

—Muhammad Ali

We fall from womb to tomb, from one blackness
and toward another, remembering little of the
one and knowing nothing of the other . . . except
through faith.

—Stephen King, *Danse Macabre*

The authentic self is the soul made visible.

—Sarah Ban Breathnach

Life—a spiritual pickle preserving the body
from decay.

—Ambrose Bierce

Man chooses either life or death, but he chooses;
everything he does, from going to the toilet to
mathematical speculation, is an act of religious
worship, either of God or of himself.

—W. H. Auden

Even if you are a minority of one, the truth is
the truth.

—Mahatma Gandhi

If they drive God from the earth, we shall shelter Him underground.

—Fyodor Dostoevsky, *The Brothers Karamazov*

To believe in a God means to see that the facts of the world are not the end of the matter. To believe in God means to see that life has a meaning.

—Ludwig Wittgenstein

The finest emotion of which we are capable is the mystic emotion. Herein lies the germ of all art and all true science.

—Albert Einstein

The spirit of man is more important than mere physical strength, and the spiritual fiber of a nation than its wealth.

—Dwight D. Eisenhower

It was a great thing to open the eyes of a blind man, but it is a greater thing to open the eyes of a blind soul.

—Abbott Eliot Kittredge

For what shall it profit a man, if he shall gain the whole world, and lose his own soul?

—Jesus Christ, *The Holy Bible,* Mark 8:36

TO BEGIN

I focus on spiritual wealth now, and I'm busier, more enthusiastic, and more joyful than I have ever been.

—John Templeton

Whatever answers faith gives…such answers always give an infinite meaning to the finite existence of man; a meaning that is not destroyed by suffering, deprivation or death. This means only in faith can we find the meaning and possibility of life.

—Leo Tolstoy

Man's law changes with his understanding of man. Only the laws of the spirit remain always the same.

—Crow proverb

A man loses his fortune; he gains earnestness.
His eyesight goes; it leads him to a spirituality...
We think we are pushing our own way bravely,
but there is a great Hand in ours all the time.

—Arthur Conan Doyle

To me, spirituality means "no matter what." One stays
on the path, one commits to love, one does one's
work; one follows one's dream...no matter what.

—Yehuda Berg

There are only two ways to live your life. One is as
though nothing is a miracle. The other is as though
everything is a miracle.

—Albert Einstein

Why, who makes much of a miracle?
As to me I know of nothing else but miracles. . .

> —Walt Whitman, "Miracles"

Religion is, in reality, living. Our religion is not what
we profess, or what we say, or what we proclaim;
our religion is what we do, what we desire, what
we seek, what we dream about, what we fantasize,
what we think—all these things.

> —Jack D. Forbes

Life is either a daring adventure or nothing.

> —Helen Keller

21

Learning how to operate a soul figures to take time.

—Timothy Leary

If you look the right way, you can see that the whole world is a garden.

—Frances Hodgson Burnett, *The Secret Garden*

We are all in the gutter, but some of us are looking at the stars.

—Oscar Wilde, *Lady Windermere's Fan*

To live is the rarest thing in the world. Most people exist, that is all.

—Oscar Wilde

TO BEGIN

I find hope in the darkest of days, and focus in the brightest. I do not judge the universe.

—The Dalai Lama

Living in a world such as this is like dancing on a live volcano.

—Kentetsu Takamori

Lovely snowflakes!
Each one falls in the appropriate place.

—Zen saying

How mysterious this life was, how deep and muddy its waters ran, yet how clear and noble what emerged from them.

—Herman Hesse, *Narcissus and Goldmund*

As belief shrinks from this world, it is more necessary than ever that someone believe. Wild-eyed men in caves. Nuns in black. Monks who do not speak. We are left to believe…Hell is when no one believes.

—Don Delillo, *White Noise*

There are a thousand thousand reasons to live this life, everyone of them sufficient.

—Marilynne Robinson, *Gilead*

God asks no man whether he will accept life. That is not the choice. You must accept it. The only choice is how.

—Henry Ward Beecher

THE SPIRITUAL IN THE MATERIAL

The secular world is full of holes. We have secularized badly.

—Alain de Botton

The secular world is more spiritual than it thinks, just as the ecclesiastical world is more materialist than it cares to acknowledge.

—Lionel Blue

The real crisis we face today is a spiritual one; at root, it is a test of moral will and faith.

—Ronald Reagan

When all the trees have been cut down,
when all the animals have been hunted,
when all the waters are polluted,
when all the air is unsafe to breathe,
only then will you discover you cannot eat money.

—Native American wisdom

Many people are so poor that the only thing they have is money.

—Rodolfo Costa

The Spiritual in the Material

Lives with no more sense of spiritual meaning than
that provided by shopping malls, ordinary television,
and stagnant workplaces are barren lives indeed.

—Marianne Williamson

We do whatever we can to deny intuition of the
invisible realms. We clog up our senses with
smog, jam our minds with media overload. We
drown ourselves in alcohol or medicate ourselves
into rigidly artificial states… we take pride in our
cynicism and detachment. Perhaps we are terrified
to discover that our "rationality" is itself a kind
of faith, an artifice, that beneath it lies the vast
territory of the unknown.

—Daniel Pinchbeck

God is dead not because He doesn't exist, but because we live, play, procreate, govern, and die as though He doesn't.

—Charles Colson

Our Generation has had no Great war, no Great Depression. Our war is spiritual. Our depression is our lives.

—Chuck Palahniuk

We are looking to brands for poetry and for spirituality, because we're not getting those things from our communities or from each other.

—Naomi Klein

Our scientific power has outrun our spiritual power.
We have guided missiles and misguided men.

—Martin Luther King, Jr.

Science only goes so far, then comes God.

—Nicholas Sparks, *The Notebook*

I'm not going to fight in the physical with physical
weapons, because it's not a physical fight. I'm
going to fight with spiritual weapons, cause it's a
spiritual fight.

—Stephen Baldwin

31

My choosing Islam was not a political statement; it was a spiritual statement.

—Kareem Abdul-Jabbar, American professional basketball player

A depressing number of people seem to process everything literally. They are to wit as a blind man is to a forest, able to find every tree, but each one coming as a surprise.

—Roger Ebert

We need to remember that we are spiritual beings spending some time in a human body.

—Barbara De Angelis

We are all connected; to each other, biologically.
To the earth, chemically. To the rest of the universe
atomically.

—Neil deGrasse Tyson

I read somewhere that some people believe that
the entire universe is a matrix of living thought. And
I said, "Man, if that's not a definition of God, I don't
know what is."

—Alan Arkin

Mathematics is the language in which God wrote
the universe.

—Galileo Galilei

Science investigates; religion interprets. Science gives man knowledge, which is power; religion gives man wisdom, which is control… The two are not rivals.

—Martin Luther King, Jr.

God created everything by number, weight and measure.

—Isaac Newton

I believe in Darwin and God together.

—Ray Bradbury

Science is not only compatible with spirituality; it is a profound source of spirituality.

—Carl Sagan

As for science and religion, the known and admitted facts are few and plain enough. All that the parsons say is unproved. All that the doctors say is disproved. That's the only difference between science and religion…

—G. K. Chesterton

Science and religion are not at odds. Science is simply too young to understand.

—Dan Brown, *Angels & Demons*

35

I simply believe that some part of the human Self or Soul is not subject to the laws of space and time.

—Carl Jung

Even a speck of dust is pervaded by divinity.

—Baal Shem Tov

We are not human beings having a spiritual experience. We are spiritual beings having a human experience.

—Pierre Teilhard de Chardin

My religion consists of a humble admiration of the illimitable superior spirit who reveals himself in the slight details we are able to perceive with our frail and feeble mind.

—Albert Einstein

Every natural fact is a symbol of some spiritual fact.

—Ralph Waldo Emerson

The language of God is not English or Latin; the language of God is cellular and molecular.

—Timothy Leary

Science brings men nearer to God.

—Louis Pasteur

Everyone who is seriously engaged in the pursuit of science becomes convinced that the laws of nature manifest the existence of a spirit vastly superior to that of men.

—Albert Einstein

I do feel that evolution is being controlled by some sort of divine engineer.

—Kurt Vonnegut

When you study natural science and the miracles of creation, if you don't turn into a mystic you are not a natural scientist.

—Albert Hofmann

If you don't know what's meant by God, watch a forsythia branch or a lettuce leaf sprout.

—Martin F. Fischer

This most beautiful system of the sun, planets, and comets could only proceed from the counsel and dominion of an intelligent and powerful Being.

—Isaac Newton

39

The facts of life do not penetrate to the sphere
in which our beliefs are cherished; they did not
engender those beliefs, and they are powerless to
destroy them.

—Marcel Proust, *Swann's Way*

The universe shows us the life of God, or rather
it is in itself the life of God. . . . God is not out of
the universe any more than the universe is out
of God. God is the principle, the universe is the
consequence.

—Henri-Dominique Lacordaire

Nature only shows us the tail of the lion. I am convinced, however, that the lion is attached to it, even though he cannot reveal himself directly because of his enormous size.

—Albert Einstein

To believe in a God means to see that the facts of the world are not the end of the matter.

—Ludwig Wittgenstein

Rational thinking which is free from assumptions ends therefore in mysticism.

—Albert Schweitzer

In want of other proofs, the thumb would convince me of the existence of a God.

—Isaac Newton

Faith is different from proof; the latter is human, the former is a Gift from God.

—Blaise Pascal

Each human life is unique, born of a miracle that reaches beyond laboratory science.

—Bill Clinton

The Spiritual in the Material

I don't understand why people insist on pitting
concepts of evolution and creation against each
other. Why can't they see that spiritualism and
science are one? That bodies evolve and souls
evolve and the universe is a fluid package that
marries them both in a wonderful package called a
human being.

—Garth Stein, *The Art of Racing in the Rain*

Spirituality leaps where science cannot yet follow,
because science must always test and measure,
and much of reality and human experience is
immeasurable.

—Starhawk

We are more than just flesh and bones. There's a certain spiritual nature and something of the mind that we can't measure. . . . With all our sophisticated equipment, we cannot monitor or define it, and yet it's there.

—Benjamin Carson

Human spirituality is to seek an answer to the question: "how can you make sense out of a world which does not seem to be intrinsically reasonable?"

—John D. Morgan

Scientists have calculated that the chance of anything so patently absurd actually existing are millions to one. But magicians have calculated that million-to-one chances crop up nine times out of ten.

—Terry Pratchet, *Mort*, describing the origin myth of the Discworld

Whether you take the doughnut hole as a blank space or as an entity unto itself is a purely metaphysical question and does not affect the taste of the doughnut one bit.

—Haruki Murakami, *A Wild Sheep Chase*

45

I believe in God, only I spell it "Nature."

—Frank Lloyd Wright

Be still, my heart, these great trees are prayers.

—Rabindranath Tagore

All actual life is encounter.

—Martin Buber

Those who know God know that it is quite a mistake to suppose that there are only five senses.

—Coventry Patmore

47

Some people feel the rain. Others just get wet.

—Roger Miller

The most beautiful emotion we can experience is the mysterious. It is the fundamental emotion that stands at the cradle of all true art and science.

—Albert Einstein

The possession of knowledge does not kill the sense of wonder and mystery. There is always more mystery.

—Anaïs Nin

48

We all have a thirst for wonder. It's a deeply human quality. Science and religion are both bound up with it. What I'm saying is, you don't have to make stories up…

—Carl Sagan

You see, when weaving a blanket, an Indian woman leaves a flaw in the weaving of that blanket to let the soul out.

—Martha Graham

Why do you hasten to remove anything which hurts your eye, while if something affects your soul you postpone the cure until next year?

—Horace

We fear men so much, because we fear God so little.

—William Gurnall

A man who recognizes no God is probably placing an inordinate value on himself.

—Robertson Davies

The Spiritual in the Material

Sometimes you struggle so hard to feed your family one way, you forget to feed them the other way, with spiritual nourishment. Everybody needs that.

—James Brown

I still have a spiritual base and a spiritual foundation...I pray for humility, honestly, because it's very easy to be caught up in this world.

—Katy Perry

Man's essential idea is spirit and we must not allow ourselves to be put off by the fact that he is also able to walk on two legs.

— Søren Kierkegaard

51

Science seems to me to teach in the highest and strongest manner the great truth . . . of entire surrender to the will of God. Sit down before fact as a little child, be prepared to give up every preconceived notion, follow humbly wherever and to whatever abyss nature leads, or you shall learn nothing.

—Thomas Huxley

We do not need more intellectual power, we need more spiritual power. We do not need more of the things that are seen, we need more of the things that are unseen.

—Calvin Coolidge

"What do you think of God," the teacher asked. After a pause, the young pupil replied, "He's not a think, he's a feel."

—Paul Frost

A spiritually illumined soul lives in the world, yet is never contaminated by it.

—Swami Bhaskarananda

There's wonder and awe enough in the real world.
Nature's a lot better at inventing wonders than we are.

—Carl Sagan

Heaven cannot but be high. Earth cannot but be
broad. The sun and moon cannot but revolve. All
creation cannot but flourish. To do so is their TAO.

—Zhuangzi

54

I understand once again that the greatness of God always reveals itself in the simple things.

—Paulo Coelho, *Like the Flowing River*

The spiritual life does not remove us from the world but leads us deeper into it.

—Henri J. M. Nouwen

If I discover within myself a desire which no experience in this world can satisfy, the most probable explanation is that I was made for another world.

—C. S. Lewis

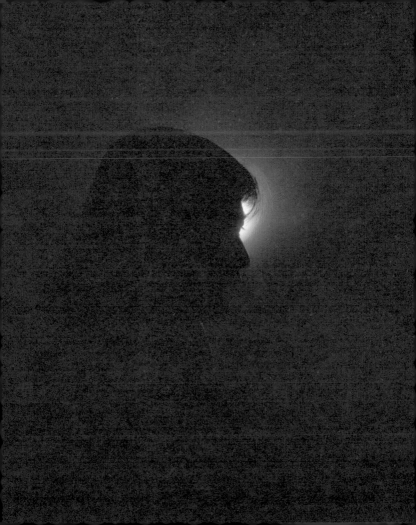

FAITH AND DOUBT

That is what faith is: God perceived by the heart, not by the reason.

—Blaise Pascal

Now faith is the substance of things hoped for, the evidence of things not seen.

—*The Holy Bible*, Hebrews 11:1-3

Faith is an act of a finite being who is grasped by, and turned to, the infinite.

—Paul Tillich

Faith is the subtle chain
That binds us to the Infinite.

—Elizabeth Oakes Smith

To eat bread without hope is still slowly to
starve to death.

—Pearl S. Buck

Take the first step in faith. You don't have to see the
whole staircase, just take the first step.

—Martin Luther King, Jr.

Faith and Doubt

A rock pile ceases to be a rock pile the moment a
single man contemplates it, bearing within him the
image of a cathedral.

—Antoine de Saint-Exupéry, *The Little Prince*

You block your dream when you allow your fear to
grow bigger than your faith.

—Mary Manin Morrissey

The way to see by faith is to shut the eye of reason.

—Benjamin Franklin

Faith is a higher faculty than reason.

—Philip James Bailey

Faith consists in believing when it is beyond the power of reason to believe.

—Voltaire

Exactly at the instant when hope ceases to be reasonable it begins to be useful.

—G. K. Chesterton

It's a sad and unfortunate state of affairs . . . to live in a world where eight-year-olds refuse to believe in anything that they cannot touch or measure, and anyone who happens to see a thing that is invisible to most people is immediately branded a lunatic.

—Caitlín R. Kiernan

I heard once of an American who so defined faith,
"that faculty which enables us to believe things
which we know to be untrue." . . . He meant that
we shall have an open mind, and not let a little bit of
truth check the rush of the big truth.

—Abraham Van Helsing, in Bram Stoker's *Dracula*

I believe that faith is a precursor of all our ideas.
Without faith, there never could have evolved
hypothesis, theory, science or mathematics.

—Charlie Chaplin

You can't know, you can only believe—or not.

—C. S. Lewis

61

That's the thing about faith. If you don't have it,
you can't understand it. And if you do,
no explanation is necessary.

—Major Kira Nerys, *Star Trek: Deep Space Nine*

Seeing is not believing. Believing is seeing! You see
things, not as they are, but as you are.

—Eric Butterworth

Faith has to do with things that are not seen, and
hope with things that are not in hand.

—St. Thomas Aquinas

To disbelieve is easy; to scoff is simple; to have faith is harder.

—Louis L' Amour

Belief consists in accepting the affirmations of the soul; unbelief, in denying them.

—Ralph Waldo Emerson

Faith is believing what you know ain't so.

—Mark Twain

Faith is the daring of the soul to go farther than it can see.

—William Newton Clarke

Faith and Doubt

We can approach belief from an intellectual path,
but in the end, God must be taken on faith. Proofs
are for things of this world, things in time and of
time, not beyond time.

—Dean Koontz, *Brother Odd*

I now understand the need for faith—pure, blind,
fly-in-the-face-of-reason faith—as a small life
preserver in the wild and endless sea of a universe
ruled by unfeeling laws . . .

—Dan Simmons, *Hyperion*

All I have seen teaches me to trust the Creator for
all I have not seen.

—Ralph Waldo Emerson

Sometimes the most real things in the world are the things you can't see.

—Conductor, *The Polar Express*

Truly I say to you, if you have faith, and do not doubt . . . if you say to this mountain, "Be taken up and cast into the sea," it shall happen.

—Jesus Christ, *The Holy Bible*, Matthew 21:21

The only thing wrong with love and faith and belief is not having it.

—Haley James Scott, *One Tree Hill*

What good is faith if we don't use it?

—Catherine Weaver, *Terminator:
The Sarah Connor Chronicles*

Kindness is a mark of faith, and whoever has not
kindness has not faith.

—The Prophet Muhammad

Sometimes you just have to jump out the window
and grow wings on the way down.

—Ray Bradbury

In faith there is enough light for those who want to believe and enough shadows to blind those who don't.

—Blaise Pascal

Truth is the torch that gleams through the fog without dispelling it.

—Claude-Adrien Helvetius

A belief which leaves no place for doubt is not a belief; it is a superstition.

—José Bergamín

Faith and Doubt

Doubt is useful, it keeps faith a living thing. After all, you cannot know the strength of your faith until it has been tested.

—Pi Patel, *Life of Pi*

Doubt isn't the opposite of faith; it is an element of faith.

—Paul Tillich

Faith doesn't mean that you don't have doubts.

—Barack Obama

Only in a world where faith is difficult can faith exist.

—Lee Strobel

It is not as a child that I believe and confess Jesus Christ. My hosanna is born of a furnace of doubt.

—Fyodor Dostoevsky

At the bottom of great doubt lies great awakening.

—Hakuin

If you have any faith, give me, for heaven's sake, a share of it! Your doubts you may keep to yourself, for I have a plenty of my own.

—Johann Wolfgang von Goethe

Mirror of constant faith, revered and mourn'd!

—Homer, *The Odyssey*

Faith and Doubt

If a man will begin with certainties, he shall end
in doubts; but if he will be content to begin with
doubts, he shall end in certainties.

—Francis Bacon

Faith is, at one and the same time, absolutely
necessary and altogether impossible.

—Stanisław Lem

Never underestimate the power of blind faith. It
manifests in ways that bend the laws of physics, or
breaks them entirely.

—Sophie-Anne, *True Blood*

It's not about making sense. It's about believing in something, and letting that belief be real enough to change your life. . . . You don't fix faith . . . it fixes you.

—Shepherd Book, *Firefly*

It doesn't have to make sense. It's faith, it's faith. It's the flower of light in the field of darkness that's giving me the strength to carry on.

—Eli, *The Book of Eli*

At the end of the day, faith is a funny thing. It turns up when you don't really expect it.

—Dr. Meredith Grey, *Grey's Anatomy*

Faith and Doubt

None of us knows what might happen even the next minute, yet still we go forward. Because we trust. Because we have Faith.

—Paulo Coelho, *Brida*

There lives more faith in honest doubt, believe me, than in half the creeds.

—Alfred Tennyson

Faith is something that cannot be won through intimidation and fear.

—Osiric, *Stargate SG-1*

I would like the church to be a place where the questions of people are honored rather than a place where we have all the answers.

—Bishop John Shelby Spong

Doubt is not always a sign that a man is wrong; it may be a sign that he is thinking.

—Oswald Chambers

Faith . . . is the art of holding on to things your reason has once accepted in spite of your changing moods.

—C. S. Lewis, *Mere Christianity*

But as the most beautiful light is born of darkness, so the faith which springs from conflict is often the strongest and the best.

—Robert Turnbull

Faith says, "I am certain, not because feeling testifies to it, but because God says it."

—Bernard Mandeville

The atheists have the greatest faith: they believe that God does not exist.

—Andrzej Majewski

I don't personally have enough faith to be
an atheist.

—Rick Warren

The highest praise of God consists in the denial of
him by the athiest who finds creation so perfect
that it can dispense with a creator.

—Marcel Proust, *The Guermantes Way*

Faith is not about having the right answers, . . .
Faith is a hunch . . . that there is something bigger . . .
connecting us all together.

—Father Brian Kilkenney Finn, *Keeping the Faith*

Faith and Doubt

Faith is not something to grasp, it is a state to grow into.

—Mahatma Gandhi

Faith—is the Pierless Bridge
Supporting what We see
Unto the Scene that We do not.

—Emily Dickinson

To my mind, faith is like being in the sun. When you are in the sun, can you avoid creating a shadow?
. . . You can't. This shadow is doubt. And it goes wherever you go as long as you stay in the sun. And who wouldn't want to be in the sun?

—Yann Martel, *Beatrice & Virgil*

Because you have seen me, you have believed;
blessed are those who have not seen and yet
have believed.

—Jesus Christ, *The Holy Bible*, John 20:29,
appearing to his disciples after his resurrection

As your faith is strengthened you will find that there
is no longer the need to have a sense of control,
that things will flow as they will, and that you will
flow with them.

—Emmanuel Teney

A speculative faith consists only in the assent of the
understanding, but in a saving faith there is also the
consent of the heart.

—Jonathan Edwards

Faith and Doubt

Faith sees God's face in every human face.

—Catherine Doherty

He who loves God without faith reflects upon
himself; he who loves God in faith reflects
upon God.

— Søren Kierkegaard

Faith does not need to push the river because
faith is able to trust that there is a river. The river is
flowing. We are in it.

—Richard Rohr

Faith creates the foundation for conviction.

—Simon Soloveychik

Faith is not just something you have, it's something you do.

—Barack Obama

I would rather live my life as if there is a God and die to find out there isn't, than live my life as if there isn't and die to find out there is.

—Albert Camus

For me, there is no hope without faith. Faith in a higher good. Faith in our divinity.

—Alyssa Milano

Faith is the force of life.

—Leo Tolstoy

Faith and Doubt

If you only believe when it's easy, you don't
really believe.

—Laurell K. Hamilton

A belief is not true because it is useful.

—Henri-Frédéric Amiel

Any faith that must be supported by the evidence of
the senses is not real faith.

—A. W. Tozer

Faith is what makes life bearable, with all its
tragedies and ambiguities and sudden, startling joys.

—Madeleine L'Engle

I dont think that we're meant to understand it all the time. I think that sometimes we just have to have faith.

—Nicholas Sparks, *A Walk to Remember*

To have faith is to trust yourself to the water. When you swim you don't grab hold of the water, because if you do you will sink and drown. Instead you relax, and float.

—Alan Wilson Watts

Faith is not Desire. Faith is Will. Desires are things that need to be satisfied, whereas Will is a force. Will changes the space around us . . .

—Paulo Coelho, *The Witch Of Portobello*

Faith and Doubt

Our faith begins at the point where atheists
suppose it must be at an end.

—Hans Joachim Iwand

I never needed eyes to see—never. I simply needed
vision and belief.

—Caroline Casey

I shut my eyes in order to see.

—Paul Gaugin

The very essence of romance is uncertainty.

—Oscar Wilde

Faith is reason grown courageous.

—Sherwood Eddy

Since living is believing, no one can be completely lacking in faith.

—Kentetsu Takamori

Some things have to be believed to be seen.

—Madeleine L'Engle

RELIGION VS. SPIRITUALITY

Perhaps not one religion contains all of the truth of the world. Perhaps every religion contains fragments of the truth, and it is our responsibility to identify those fragments and piece them together.

—Christopher Paolini, *Brisingr*

It is a mistake to suppose that God is only, or even chiefly, concerned with religion.

—William Temple

Anyone who thinks sitting in church can make you a Christian must also think that sitting in a garage can make you a car.

—Garrison Keillor

If organized religion has become less relevant, it's not because churches have held fast to their creedal beliefs—it's because they've held fast to their conventional structures, programs, roles and routines.

—Gary Hamel

God has no religion.

—Henry Whitney Bellows

I believe in God, but not as one thing, not as an old man in the sky. I believe that what people call God is something in all of us. I believe that what Jesus and Mohammed and Buddha and all the rest said was right. It's just that the translations have gone wrong.

—John Lennon

True religion is the life we lead, not the creed we profess.

—Louis Nizer

The Christian does not think God will love us because we are good, but that God will make us good because He loves us.

—C. S. Lewis

The moment we attempt to organize mysticism, we destroy its essence. Religion, then, is mysticism in which the mystical has been killed.

—Tom Robbins

Do you really think, as some have argued, that God will be saying: "You know, that guy, the Dalai Lama, is not bad. What a pity he's not a Christian"? I don't think that is the case—because, you see, God is not a Christian.

—Desmond Tutu

I don't like religion much, and I am glad that in the Bible the word is not to be found.

—Martin Buber

It makes a great deal of difference what sort of God men believe in.

—Henry Ward Beecher

God is not the name of God, but an opinion about Him.

—Pope Xystus I

There are just some kind of men who—who're so busy worrying about the next world they've never learned to live in this one, and you can look down the street and see the results.

—Harper Lee, *To Kill a Mockingbird*

The true meaning of religion is thus not simply morality, but morality touched by emotion.

—Matthew Arnold

Religion in so far as it is a source of consolation is a hindrance to true faith.

—Simone Weil

Religion Vs. Spirituality

We have just enough religion to make us hate, but not enough to make us love one another.

—Jonathan Swift

If this is going to be a Christian nation that doesn't help the poor, either we have to pretend that Jesus was just as selfish as we are, or we've got to acknowledge that He commanded us to love the poor…without condition and then admit that we just don't want to do it.

—Stephen Colbert

Religion. It's given people hope in a world torn apart by religion.

—Jon Stewart

Every day, people are straying away from the church and going back to God.

—Lenny Bruce

If there is a God, atheism must seem to Him as less of an insult than religion.

—Edmond de Goncourt

God save us from religion.

—David Eddings

Any religion is a shadow of God. But the shadows of God are not God.

—Margaret Atwood, *The Year of the Flood*

94

I think of religions as franchise operations. Like chicken franchise operations. But that doesn't mean there's no chicken, right?

—William Gibson

Religion is for people who are scared to go to hell. Spirituality is for people who have already been there.

—Bonnie Raitt

I would describe my spirituality as exactly the opposite of having a religious affiliation.

—Bill Maher

95

Say nothing of my religion. It is known to God and myself alone. Its evidence before the world is to be sought in my life: if it has been honest and dutiful to society the religion which has regulated it cannot be a bad one.

—Thomas Jefferson

Religion can be both good and bad—it is spirituality that counts.

—Pat Buckley

I'm not religious, but I'm very spiritual.

—Paul McCartney

How many observe Christ's birthday! How few, His precepts!

—Benjamin Franklin

Being privately spiritual but not religious just doesn't interest me. There is nothing challenging about having deep thoughts all by oneself.

—Lillian Daniel

My atheism, like that of Spinoza, is true piety towards the universe and denies only gods fashioned by men in their own image to be servants of their human interests.

—George Santayana

Make sure that your religion is a matter between you and God only.

—Ludwig Wittgenstein

Some men want to have religion like a dark lantern, and carry it in their pocket, where nobody but themselves can get any good from it.

—Henry Ward Beecher

This is a dangerous idea I've put on the table: my God vs. your God, their God vs. our God . . . vs. no God. It is very easy, in these times, to see religion as a force for division rather than unity.

—Bono

Live a good life. If there are gods and they are just, then they will not care how devout you have been, but will welcome you based on the virtues you have lived by.

—Marcus Aurelius

No one is without Christianity, if we agree on what we mean by that word. It is every individual's individual code of behavior by means of which he makes himself a better human being than his nature wants to be.

—William Faulkner

We spend all our time looking for some concept of Truth, but Truth is what is left when we drop all concepts.

—David Merzel

Just because I don't have nothin' to pass around for people to put money in a bucket don't mean I ain't doing God's work.

—Tupac Shakur

I don't know how your theology works, but if Jesus has a choice between stained glass windows and feeding starving kids in Haiti, I have a feeling he'd choose the starving kids in Haiti.

—Tony Campolo

I learned that religion is often the enemy of God . . . religion is the artifice, you know, the building, after God has left it sometimes . . . I think what God is interested in is people's hearts.

—Bono

God wants spiritual fruit, not religious nuts.

—A church signboard in New York City

Christianity does not consist in a proud priesthood, a costly church, an imposing ritual, a fashionable throng, a pealing organ . . . but in the spirit of filial trust in God, and ardent, impartial, overflowing love to man.

—T. J. Mumford

This is my simple religion. There is no need for
temples; no need for complicated philosophy.
Our own brain, our own heart is our temple; the
philosophy is kindness.

—The Dalai Lama

The only true mosque is that in the heart of saints.
The mosque that is built in the hearts of the saints
is the place of worship for all, for God dwells there.

—Rumi, *The Masnavi*, Book 2 Story 13

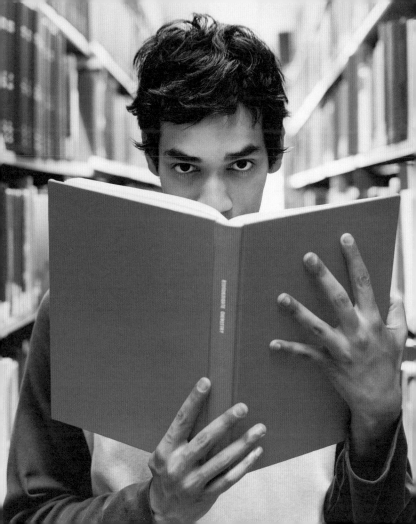

THE QUEST TO KNOW

The most important question a human being has to face . . . What is it? The question, Why are we here?

—Elie Wiesel

Human spirituality is to seek an answer to the question: "how can you make sense out of a world which does not seem to be intrinsically reasonable?"

—John D. Morgan

The wonderful thing is that the soul already knows . . . that there is something behind the veil, . . . that there is something to be sought for in the highest spheres of life, that there is some beauty to be seen, that there is someone to be known who is knowable.

—Hazrat Inayat Khan

I want to know how God created this world. I'm not interested in this or that phenomenon, in the spectrum of this or that element. I want to know His thoughts, the rest are details.

—Albert Einstein

Heaven is satisfied curiosity.

—Paola Antonelli

Those afraid of the universe as it really is . . . and envision a Cosmos centered on human beings will prefer the fleeting comforts of superstition. They avoid rather than confront the world. But those with the courage to explore the weave and structure of the Cosmos, even where it differs profoundly from their wishes and prejudices, will penetrate its deepest mysteries.

—Carl Sagan

I have become so accustomed to think "scientifically" that I am afraid even to imagine that there may be something else beyond the outer covering of life.

—P. D. Ouspensky

If you ask me what I want to achieve, it's to create an awareness, which is already the beginning of teaching.

—Elie Wiesel

Wonder is the beginning of wisdom.

—Socrates

Wisdom is a sacred communion.

—Victor Hugo

To study and not think is a waste. To think and not study is dangerous.

—Confucius

It's that moment, that brief epiphany when the universe opens up and shows us something, and in that instant we get just a sense of an order greater than Heaven and, as yet at least, beyond the grasp of Stephen Hawking.

—Terry Pratchett

By three methods we may learn wisdom: first, by reflection, which is noblest; second, by imitation, which is easiest; and third, by experience, which is the most bitter.

—Confucius

We don't receive wisdom; we must discover it for
ourselves after a journey that no one can take for us
or spare us.

—Marcel Proust

For in their hearts doth Nature stir them so
Then people long on pilgrimage to go
And palmers to be seeking foreign strands
To distant shrines renowned in sundry lands.

—Geoffrey Chaucer, *The Canterbury Tales*

My favorite thing to do is to go where I've
never been.

—Diane Arbus

The Quest to Know

Pilgrims are poets who create by taking journeys.

—Richard R. Niebuhr

The beginning of wisdom is found in doubting;
By doubting we come to the question, and by
seeking we may come upon the truth.

—Pierre Abelard

Doubt grows with knowledge.

—Johann Wolfgang von Goethe

A thorough knowledge of the Bible is worth more
than a college education.

—Theodore Roosevelt

111

Know why you believe, understand what you believe, and possess a reason for the faith that is in you.

—Frances Wright

There are many paths to God, my son. I hope yours will not be too difficult.

—Balthaser, *Ben-Hur*

Faith is like a toothbrush. Every person should have one and use it regularly, but he shouldn't try to use someone else's.

—J. G. Stipe

There is only one religion, although there are a hundred versions of it.

—George Bernard Shaw

Just because I'm on a different path doesn't mean I'm lost.

—Anonymous

I still believe in God. I just think there's another path to him, or her.

—Lisa Simpson, *The Simpsons*

The world is not a prison house, but a kind of spiritual kindergarten where millions of bewildered infants are trying to spell God with the wrong blocks.

—Edwin Arlington Robinson

If you think God's there, He is. If you don't, He isn't. And if that's what God's like, I wouldn't worry about it.

—Haruki Murakami, *Kafka on the Shore*

But your spiritual teachers caution you against enquiry . . . by their own creed you hold your reason from their God. Go! ask them why he gave it.

—Frances Wright

The Quest to Know

Question with boldness even the existence of
a god; because, if there be one, he must more
approve the homage of reason, than that of
blindfolded fear.

—Thomas Jefferson

We don't see things as they are, we see them as
we are.

—Anaïs Nin

"Truth" and the search for truth are no trivial matter;
and if a person goes about searching in too human
a fashion, I'll bet he won't find anything!

—Friedrich Nietzsche

Truth is ever to be found in simplicity, and not in the multiplicity and confusion of things.

—Isaac Newton

To believe there is a God is to believe the existence of all possible Good and Perfection in the Universe.

—Benjamin Whichcote

Machines never come with any extra parts, you know. They always come with the exact amount they need. So, I figured that if the entire world was one big machine, I couldn't be an extra part. I had to be here for some reason.

—Hugo Cabret, *Hugo*

Atheism turns out to be too simple. If the whole universe has no meaning, we should never have found out that it has no meaning.

—C. S. Lewis

Sometimes the questions are complicated and the answers are simple.

—Dr. Seuss

It is not the answer that enlightens, but the question.

—Eugène Ionesco

Nothing is so firmly believed as that which we least know.

—Michel de Montaigne

There's always fear of the unknown where there's mystery. It's possible to achieve a state where you realize the truth of life and fear disappears, and a lot of people have reached that state, but next to none of them are on Earth.

—David Lynch

You must accept the truth from whatever source it comes.

—Maimonides

The gods love what is mysterious, and dislike what is evident.

—*The Brihadaranyaka Upanishad*, 4.2.2.

What is known for certain is dull.

—Max Ferdinand Perutz

The riddles of God are more satisfying than the solutions of man.

—G. K. Chesterton

If we find the answer to that, it would be the ultimate triumph of human reason—for then we would know the mind of God.

—Stephen Hawking, on the possibility of answering the question of why the universe exists

I can't explain it, but spiritually it makes sense—though I don't understand how it does make sense.

—Kevin McDonald

If you're a Scientologist, you see life, things, the way they are, in all its glory, in all of its perplexity, and the more you know . . . the more you become overwhelmed by it.

—Tom Cruise

A man may fulfill the object of his existence by asking a question he cannot answer, and attempting a task he cannot achieve.

—Oliver Wendell Holmes

I hear you say "Why?" Always "Why?" You see things; and you say "Why?" But I dream things that never were; and I say "Why not?"

—George Bernard Shaw, *The Serpent*

People will do anything, no matter how absurd, in order to avoid facing their own soul.

—Carl Jung

We can easily forgive a child who is afraid of the dark; the real tragedy of life is when men are afraid of the light.

—Plato

We stumble and fall constantly even when we are most enlightened. But when we are in true spiritual darkness, we do not even know that we have fallen.

—Thomas Merton

Miracles are like pimples, because once you start looking for them, you'll find more than you ever imagined possible.

—Lemony Snicket, *The Lump of Coal*

If somebody wants a sheep, that is a proof that
one exists.

—Antoine de Saint Exupéry

Belief cannot be taught; it cannot be learned; it is
the grace of God. To affirm a belief is one thing; to
realize belief is another.

—Hazrat Inayat Khan

To know much and taste nothing—of what
use is that?

—St. Bonaventure

I can see how it might be possible for a man to look down upon the earth and be an atheist, but I cannot conceive how a man could look up into the heavens and say there is no God.

—Abraham Lincoln

I'm astounded by people who want to 'know' the universe when it's hard enough to find your way around Chinatown.

—Woody Allen

We do not know enough about the unknown to know that it is unknowable.

—G. K. Chesterton

124

When you are deluded and full of doubt, even a thousand books of scripture are not enough. When you have realized understanding, even one word is too much.

—Fen-Yang

It is said to await certainty is to await eternity.

—Jonas Salk

If you comprehend, it is not God.

—Augustine of Hippo

God is so much bigger and wiser than us, and trying to see what He's thinking would be like an ant trying to see what I'm thinking.

—Dewey, *Malcolm in the Middle*

. . . we have not yet conjectured the words, the definitions, the etymologies, the synonyms, from the secret dictionary of God.

—Jorge Luis Borges

Every word, every image used for God is a distortion more than a description.

—Anthony de Mello

Nothing true can be said about God from a posture of defense.

—Marilynne Robinson, *Gilead*

The truth does not change according to our ability to stomach it.

—Flannery O'Connor

He that will believe only what he can fully comprehend, must have a very long head, or a very short creed.

—Charles Caleb Colton

For those who believe, no explanation is necessary; for those who do not believe, no explanation is possible.

—Franz Werfel

My years as a mystic have made me question almost all my assumptions. They've made me a proud I-don't-know-it-all.

—Elizabeth Lesser

For all that "I was lost, I am found," it is probably more accurate to say, "I was really lost, I'm a little less so at the moment."

—Bono

129

You who want knowledge,
seek the Oneness
within
There you
will find
the clear mirror
already waiting

—Hadewijich II

I believe that we do not know anything for certain,
but everything probably.

—Christiaan

The doorstep to the temple of wisdom is a
knowledge of our own ignorance.

—Benjamin Franklin

Never mistake knowledge for wisdom. One helps
you make a living; the other helps you make a life.

—Sandra Carey

We don't choose the things we believe in; they
choose us.

—Lamar Burgess, *Minority Report*

The belief that God will do everything for man is as
untenable as the belief that man can do everything
for himself.

—Martin Luther King, Jr.

The great act of faith is when a man decides that he is not God.

—Olivia Wendell Holmes

Begin by regarding every thing from a moral point of view, and you will end by believing in God.

—Thomas Arnold

Go to the truth beyond the mind. Love is the bridge.

—Stephen Levine

A person cannot approach the divine by reaching beyond the human. To become human, is what this individual person, has been created for.

—Martin Buber

The best way to know God is to love many things.

—Vincent Van Gogh

He who believes needs no explanation.

—Euripides, *The Bacchae*

You can only find truth with logic if you have already found truth without it.

—G. K. Chesterton

I know now, Lord, why you utter no answer. You are yourself the answer. Before your face questions die away. What other answer would suffice?

—C. S. Lewis

133

If you do not believe in a personal God, the
question: "What is the purpose of life?" is
unaskable and unanswerable.

—J. R. R. Tolkien

If you stumble at mere believability, what are you
living for? Isn't love hard to believe?

—Yann Martel, *Life of Pi*

There's no black and white, left and right to me anymore; there's only up and down and down is very close to the ground. And I'm trying to go up . . .

—Bob Dylan

The question of immortality is . . . not a scholarly question. It is a question welling up from the interior which the subject must put to itself as it becomes conscious of itself.

—Søren Kierkegaard

We're all lonely for something we don't know we're lonely for. How else to explain the curious feeling that goes around feeling like missing somebody we've never even met?

—David Foster Wallace

Here is a test to find whether your mission on earth is finished: If you're alive it isn't.

—Richard Bach

The highest form of spiritual work is the realization of the essence of man. . . . You never learn the answer; you can only become the answer.

—Richard Rose

GOD AND US

I believe there is one Supreme most perfect being
. . . I believe He is pleased and delights in the
happiness of those He has created.

—Benjamin Franklin

God didn't put us here for that pat on the back. He
created us so He could be here Himself. So He could
exist in the lives of those He created in His image.

—Father Francis Mulcahy, *M*A*S*H*

Every believer is God's miracle.

—Phillip James Bailey

Through the Thou a person becomes I.

—Martin Buber

The true expression of Christian character is not in good-doing, but in God-likeness.

—Oswald Chambers

To seek God within ourselves avails us far more than to look for Him amongst creatures.

—Teresa of Avila

God and Us

It is said that God notes each sparrow that falls. And so He does . . . because the Sparrow is God. And when a cat stalks a sparrow both of them are God, carrying out God's thoughts.

—Robert A. Heinlein, *Stranger in a Strange Land*

There exists no separation between gods and men; one blends softly casual into the other.

—Frank Herbert, *Dune Messiah*

If I exist, God exists. With me it is a necessity of my being as it is with millions. They may not be able to talk about it, but from their life you can see that it is a part of their life.

—Mahatma Gandhi

The soul of God is poured into the world through the thoughts of men.

—Ralph Waldo Emerson

I think we all have a little voice inside us that will guide us. It may be God, I don't know. But I think that if we shut out all the noise and clutter from our lives and listen to that voice, it will tell us the right thing to do.

—Christopher Reeve

The word which God has written on the brow of every man is Hope.

—Victor Hugo, *Les Misérables*

God and Us

Can there be a sin which could exceed the love
of God?

—Fyodor Dostoevsky, *The Brothers Karamazov*

When Allah created his creatures He wrote above
His throne: "Verily, my Compassion overcomes
my wrath."

—*The Holy Quran*

God is love. . . . We wouldn't recognize that love.
It might even look like hate. It would be enough
to scare us—God's love. It set fire to a bush in the
desert, didn't it, and smashed open graves and set
the dead walking in the dark.

—Graham Greene

143

We need not join the mad rush to purchase an earthly fallout shelter. God is our eternal fallout shelter.

—Martin Luther King, Jr.

A man with God is always in the majority.

—John Knox

A God all mercy is a God unjust.

—Edward Young

God is in the tiger as well as in the lamb.

—John Updike, *Rabbit Redux*

The great soul that sits on the throne of the universe is not, never was, and never will be, in a hurry.

—J. G. Holland

Being God isn't easy. If you do too much, people get dependent on you. And if you do nothing, they lose hope. You have to use a light touch, like a safecracker or a pickpocket.

—God, *Futurama*

They say that God is everywhere, and yet we always think of Him as somewhat of a recluse.

—Emily Dickinson, in a letter to Mrs. J. G. Holland

I have seen that in any great undertaking it is not enough for a man to depend simply upon himself.

—Isna-la-wica

We turn to God for help when our foundations are shaking, only to learn that it is God who is shaking them.

—Charles C. West

God don't make no mistakes, that's how He got to be God.

—Archie Bunker, *All in the Family*

You cannot know God until you've stopped telling yourself that you already know God. You cannot hear God until you stop thinking you've already heard God.

—Neale Donald Walsch

God is like a barber: don't expect him to give you a haircut, you must first get at his barbershop.

—Anonymous

God has such a deep reverence for our freedom that he'd rather let us freely go to Hell than be compelled to go to Heaven.

—Desmond Tutu

No man or woman can truly choose to serve God
unless they are equally free to refuse to serve Him,
and God desires for His people to come to Him
clear-eyed and joyously, not cringing in terror of the
Inquisition and the damnation of Hell.

—David Weber

There's only one response God's got to anything
you might care to tell Him—that your brother's
dying of AIDS, for example, and that you'd really
appreciate it if He could help out with a bit of the
old razzle-dazzle—and that response is: Yeah,
I know.

—Glen Duncan, *I, Lucifer*

God and Us

God is not a cosmic bellboy for whom we can press
a button to get things done.

—Harry Emerson Fosdick

One thing I can't stand, it's people groveling.

—God, *Monty Python and the Holy Grail*

How tired God must be of guilt and loneliness, for
that is all we ever bring to Him.

—Mignon McLaughlin

God does not become weary of forgiving until the
servant becomes weary of asking for forgiveness.

—Imam al-Ghazali

God often visits us, but most of the time we are not at home.

—Joseph Roux

God is acting on your soul all the time, whether you have spiritual sensations or not.

—Evelyn Underhill

I rarely speak about God. To God yes. I protest against Him. I shout at Him. But open discourse about the qualities of God, about the problems that God imposes, theodicy, no. And yet He is there, in silence, in filigree.

—Elie Wiesel

God and Us

Without distance there is no dialogue between
the two.

—Martin Buber

God is subtle but he is not malicious.

—Albert Einstein

God's promises are like the stars; the darker the
night the brighter they shine.

—David Nicholas

Life's greatest tragedy is to lose God and not to
miss him.

—F. W. Norwood

153

I don't believe in God, but I miss him.

—Julian Barnes

We seem to think that God speaks by seconding the ideas we've already adopted, but God nearly always catches us by surprise…God tends to confound, astonish, and flabbergast.

—Sue Monk Kidd

Life is everything. Life is God. Everything changes and moves and that movement is God. And while there is life there is joy in consciousness of the divine. To love life is to love God.

—Leo Tolstoy, *War and Peace*

Look for God. Look for God like a man with his head on fire looks for water.

—Elizabeth Gilbert, *Eat, Pray, Love*

If anyone could prove to me that Christ is outside the truth, and if the truth really did exclude Christ, I should prefer to stay with Christ and not with truth.

—Fyodor Dostoevsky

My concern is not whether God is on our side; my greatest concern is to be on God's side, for God is always right.

—Abraham Lincoln

God is able to do more than man can understand.

—Thomas à Kempis

When God makes his presence felt through us, we are like the burning bush: Moses never took any heed what sort of bush it was—he only saw the brightness of the Lord.

—George Eliot, *Adam Bede*

Jesus tapped me on the shoulder and said, "Bob, why are you resisting me?" I said, "I'm not resisting You!" He said, "You gonna follow Me?" I said, "I've never thought about that before!" He said, "When you're not following Me, you're resisting Me."

—Bob Dylan

God and Us

I believe in the poetic genius of a creator who
would choose to express such unfathomable power
as a child born in "straw poverty" . . . As an artist,
I see the poetry of it. . . . That this scale of creation,
and the unfathomable universe, should describe
itself in such vulnerability, as a child.

—Bono, speaking about Jesus Christ

However many years life might last, no one could
ever wish for a better friend than God.

—Teresa of Avila

O Shepherd God, companion me on all the journeys
of my life. Dance through the darkness with me.

—Macrina Wiederkehr

. . . what counts is not the statements we make about God, but the intimacy of the relationship that we have with God.

—Kevin Hart

As truly as God is our Father, so truly is God our Mother.

—Julian of Norwich

Bright and clear mind—that we call God.

—Namboku Mizuno

God is a shower to the heart burned up with grief;
God is a sun to the face deluged with tears.

—Joseph Roux

God and Us

Oh, honey, God don't care which church you go,
long as you show up!

—Truvy Jones, *Steel Magnolias*

God only speaks to those who understand the
language.

—Albert Hofmann

As soon as we try to write the simplest sentence
about God, we find ourselves in anxious
perplexities, but when we stop trying to write about
God and talk with God, God is there and we can
talk with God.

—Kevin Hart

Every so often, late at night, I come downstairs, open one of my books, read a paragraph and say, My God. I sit there and cry because I feel that I'm not responsible for any of this. It's from God. And I'm so grateful, so, so grateful.

—Ray Bradbury

Be careful how you talk about God. He's the only God we have. If you let him go he won't come back. He won't even look back over his shoulder. And then what will you do?

—Harold Pinter, *Ashes to Ashes*

DEVOTION, PRAYER, MEDITATION

To Allah belong the east and the West:
Whithersoever ye turn, there is the presence of
Allah. For Allah is all-Pervading, all-Knowing.

—*The Holy Quran,* Surah al-Baqarah 2:115

A fish cannot drown in water,
A bird does not fall in air.
God doesn't vanish.
The fire brightens.

—Mechthild of Magdeburg

Knock, And He'll open the door
Vanish, And He'll make you shine like the sun
Fall, And He'll raise you to the heavens
Become nothing, And He'll turn you into everything.

—Rumi

To encounter the sacred is to be alive at the
deepest center of human existence.

—N. Scott Momaday

Batter my heart, three-personed God . . .

—John Donne, *Holy Sonnets* "No. 14"

Wherever you have seen God pass, mark that spot, and go and sit in that window again.

—Henry Ward Beecher

When I admire the wonders of a sunset or the beauty of the moon, my soul expands in the worship of the creator.

—Mahatma Gandhi

The world is charged with the grandeur of God. It will flame out, like shining from shook foil.

—Gerard Manley Hopkins

In the alternation between inhaling and exhaling, between heaven and earth, between Yin and Yang, holiness is forever being created.

—Herman Hesse, *The Glass Bead Game*

The sky seems to be a pure, a cooler blue, the trees a deeper green. The whole world is charged with the glory of God and I feel fire and music under my feet.

—Thomas Merton, on reading the scriptures

Every situation, every moment—is of infinite worth; for it is the representative of a whole eternity.

—Johann Wolfgang von Goethe

In the presence of infinite might and infinite
wisdom, the strength of the strongest man is
but weakness, and the keenest of mortal eyes see
but dimly.

—Theodore Roosevelt

This world is but the vestibule of an immortal life.
Every action of our lives touches on some chord
that will vibrate in eternity.

—Edwin Hubbell Chapin

We are on the planet to . . . wrap our
consciousness around the divine treasure within us
. . .

—Michael Beckwith

167

I want the presence of God Himself, or I don't want anything at all to do with religion… I want all that God has or I don't want any.

—A.W. Tozer

We rejoice, O God, that the tears of the earth keep her smiles in bloom.

—Rabindranath Tagore

How do you deny Allah and you were dead and He gave you life?

—*The Holy Quran*, Surah al-Baqarah 2:28

That Beloved has gone completely Wild—He has poured Himself into me!
I am Blissful and Drunk and Overflowing.

—Hafiz, "The Great Secret"

If we could see His goodness everywhere, His concern for us, His awareness of our needs…we just begin to fall in love with Him because He is so busy with us—you just can't resist Him.

—Mother Teresa

Once you accept the existence of God—however you define him, however you explain your relationship to him—then you are caught forever with his presence in the center of all things.

—Morris West

169

What you are is God's gift to you, what you become is your gift to God.

—Hans Urs von Balthasar

Yesterday is history, tomorrow is mystery, today is God's gift, that's why we call it the present.

—Joan Rivers

He who does not reflect his life back to God in gratitude does not know himself.

—Albert Schweitzer

The greatest honor we can give Almighty God is to live gladly because of the knowledge of his love.

—Julian of Norwich

The windows of my soul I throw
Wide open to the sun.

—John Greenleaf Whittier

God is an unutterable sigh, planted in the depths of
the soul.

—Jean Paul Richter

May the peace of God disturb you always.

—Anthony deMello

The freshness of my eyes is given to me in prayer.

—The Prophet Muhammad

171

There are thoughts which are prayers. There are
moments when, whatever the posture of the body,
the soul is on its knees.

—Victor Hugo

Prayer is the spirit speaking truth to Truth.

—Philip James Bailey

Our prayers should be for blessings in general, for
God knows best what is good for us.

—Socrates

Prayer is not asking. It is a longing of the soul. It is
daily admission of one's weakness.

—Mahatma Gandhi

172

Devotion, Prayer, Meditation

It doesn't matter how you pray—with your head
bowed in silence, or crying out in grief, or dancing.
Churches are good for prayer, but so are garages
and cars and mountains and showers and dance
floors.

—Anne Lamott

He prayeth best who loveth best
All things, both great and small.

—Samuel Taylor Coleridge

To feel the supreme and moving beauty of the
spectacle to which Nature invites her ephemeral
guests! . . . that is what I call prayer.

—Claude Debussy

173

I think what happens in a religious life is that we have those experiences of affirmation . . . Each day you say 'Yes' to that Yes.

—Kevin Hart

A culture that does not teach prayer soon runs mad with desire.

—Laurence Freeman

Praying without ceasing is not ritualized, nor are there even words.

—Peace Pilgrim

Prayer needs no speech.

—Mahatma Gandhi

It is better in prayer to have a heart without words
than words without a heart.

—Mahatma Gandhi

Prayer is not eloquence, but earnestness; not the
definition of helplessness, but the feeling of it; not
figures of speech, but compunction of soul.

—Hannah More

As in poetry, so in prayer, the whole subject matter
should be furnished by the heart.

—Edward Payson

Prayer is the pulse of the renewed soul.

—Octavius Winslow

175

We need to quit praying out of memory and start praying out of imagination.

—Mark Batterson

To pray without faith is to make a small fire while it is raining heavily.

—William Scott Downey

When a believing person prays, great things happen.

—*The Holy Bible*, James 5:13-16

O you who believe!
Seek help in patience and prayer.
Truly! Allah is with the patient.

—*The Holy Quran,* Surah al-Baqarah 2:153

Prayer is not an old woman's idle amusement.
Properly understood and applied, it is the most
potent instrument of action.

—Mahatma Gandhi

Prayer moves the hand which moves the world.

—John Aikman Wallace

To pray is to think about the meaning of life.

—Ludwig Wittgenstein

The function of prayer is not to influence God, but rather to change the nature of the one who prays.

—Søren Kierkegaard

Prayer does not fit us for the greater work; prayer is the greater work.

—Oswald Chambers

If the only prayer you ever say in your entire life is thank you, it will be enough.

—Meister Eckhart

Were there no God, we would be in this glorious world with grateful hearts and no one to thank.

—Christina Rossetti

When you do something, you should burn yourself completely, like a good bonfire, leaving no trace of yourself.

—Shunryu Suzuki

O' Great Spirit, help me always to speak the truth quietly, to listen with an open mind when others speak, and to remember the peace that may be found in silence.

—Cherokee prayer

Prayer is when you talk to God; meditation is when you listen to God.

—Diana Robinson

Silence is as deep as eternity; speech, shallow as time.

—Thomas Carlyle

In the attitude of silence the soul finds the path in a clearer light, and what is elusive and deceptive resolves itself into crystal clearness.

—Mahatma Gandhi

Stillness and tranquility set things in order in the universe.

—Lao Tzu, *Tao Te Ching*

Nothing in all creation is so like God as stillness.

—Meister Eckhart

181

The voice of the Almighty speaks most profoundly in such things as lives in silence themselves.

—Cormac McCarthy, *Blood Meridian*

Maybe God stopped appearing because He got tired of all the noise. Maybe He only appears when the world is quiet enough to pay attention.

—David Ferrando Giraut, *Journeys End in Lovers Meeting*

To make the right choices in life, you have to get in touch with your soul. To do this, you need to experience solitude, which most people are afraid of, because in the silence you hear the truth and know the solutions.

—Deepak Chopra

Solitude is the place of purification.

—Martin Buber

Doing nothing is better than being busy doing nothing.

—Lao Tzu, *Tao Te Ching*

Only in quiet waters things mirror themselves undistorted. Only in a quiet mind is adequate perception of the world.

—Hans Margolius

Do not struggle. Go with the flow of things, and you will find yourself at one with the mysterious unity of the Universe.

—Zhuangzi

Most people assume that meditation is all about stopping thoughts, getting rid of emotions, somehow controlling the mind. But actually it's . . . about stepping back, seeing the thought clearly, witnessing it coming and going.

—Andy Puddicombe

Meditation is not the menu; it's the meal.

—Victor Davich

To have nothing in mind is noble. To have no skill and no knowledge is supreme.

—Basho

Be master of mind rather than mastered by mind.

—Zen proverb

Be here now. Be someplace else later. Is that so complicated?

—David Bader

When you connect to the silence within you, that is when you can make sense of the disturbance going on around you.

—Stephen Richards

Be aware of your breathing. Notice how this takes attention away from your thinking and creates space.

—Eckhart Tolle

The more faithfully you listen to the voices within you, the better you will hear what is sounding outside.

—Dag Hammarskjöld

God speaks silently, he speaks in your heart; if your heart is noisy, chattering, you will not hear.

—Caryll Houselander

We need to find God, and He cannot be found in noise and restlessness . . . we need silence to be able to touch souls.

—Mother Teresa

Day by day become more and more intimate with the inner stillness, joy, and love which is the fragrance of your own pure heart. Keep quiet.

—Mooji

Surrender. Let silence have you. And if you find you are still swimming on the surface of the ocean, let go and sink into the depths of love.

—*Kar Kirpa Sahib*

Within each of us there is a silence, a silence as vast as the universe. And when we experience that silence, we remember who we are.

—Gunilla Norris

When I am silent, I have thunder hidden inside.

—Rumi

When the body becomes Your mirror,
how can it serve?
When the mind becomes Your mind,
what is left to remember?
Once my life is Your gesture,
how can I pray?
When all my awareness is Yours,
what can there be to know?

—Mahadeviyakka

THE MYSTICAL

Out beyond ideas of wrongdoing and rightdoing,
there is a field. I'll meet you there.

—Rumi

The whole secret of mysticism is this: that man can
understand everything by the help of what he does
not understand.

—G. K. Chesterton

The explicable requires the inexplicable. Experience
requires the nonexperienceable. The obvious
requires the mystical.

—Buckminster Fuller

Whatsoever is, is in God, and without God nothing
can be, or be conceived.

—Baruch Spinoza

God is a circle whose center is everywhere and
circumference nowhere.

—Voltaire

Kabir says: Student, tell me, what is God?
He is the breath inside the breath.

—Kabir

The Mystical

God created hand, head, and heart; the hand for the deed, the head for the world, the heart for mysticism.

—Abraham Kuyper

Mystical experiences do not necessarily supply new ideas to the mind, rather, they transform what one believes into what one knows, converting abstract concepts, such as divine love, into vivid, personal, realities.

—R. M. Jones

What is Mysticism? Is it not the attempt to draw near to God, not by rites or ceremonies, but by inward disposition?

—Florence Nightingale

We are what we think. All that we are arises with
our thoughts. With our thoughts we make the world.

—The Buddha

It moves, yet moves not.
It is far, yet It is near.
It is within all this.
And yet without all this.

—*The Isha Upanishad*

Life, like a dome of many-coloured glass,
Stains the white radiance of eternity.

—Percy Bysshe Shelley

196

The Mystical

Walk lightly in the spring; Mother Earth is pregnant.

—Kiowa proverb

Walk as if you are kissing the Earth with your feet.

—Thích Nhất Hạnh

Beauty is eternity gazing at itself in a mirror. But you are eternity and you are the mirror.

—Khalil Gibran

True mystics simply open their souls to the oncoming wave.

—Henri Bergson

The aim of the mystic is to stretch his range of consciousness as widely as possible, so that he may touch the highest pride and the deepest humility.

—Hazrat Inayat Khan

Where the philosopher guesses and argues, the mystic lives and looks . . . whilst the Absolute of the metaphysicians remains a diagram—impersonal and unattainable—the Absolute of the mystics is lovable, attainable, alive.

—Evelyn Underhill

The Mystical

Mysticism witnesses nothing but love; mysticism
is nothing but love . . . mysticism knows only that it
loves.

—Constantin Brunner

Here I sit between my brother the mountain and
my sister the sea. We three are one in loneliness,
and the love that binds us together is deep and
strong and strange.

—Khalil Gibran

Reflection is the lamp of the heart. If it departs, the
heart will have no light.

—Imam al-Haddad

When the eye becomes the heart, the heart
becomes the eye.

—Wasif Ali Wasif

What has he found who has lost God?
And what has he lost who has found God?

—Ibn 'Ata Allah al-Iskandari

Each star is a mirror reflecting the truth inside you.

—Aberjhani

But do not ask me where I am going,
As I travel in this limitless world,
Where every step I take is my home.

—Dōgen

Wherever I go, I meet myself.

—Tozan

Curving back within myself I create again and again.

—*The Bhagavad Gita*

Mysticism keeps men sane. As long as you have mystery you have health; when you destroy mystery you create morbidity.

—G. K. Chesterton

We follow the mystics. They know where they are going. They, too, go astray, but when they go astray they do so in a way that is mystical, dark, and mysterious.

—Ryszard Kapuscinski

The Word did not come into being, but it was. It did not break upon the silence, but it was older than the silence and the silence was made of it.

—N. Scott Momaday, *House Made of Dawn*

The Mystical

Remember the clear light . . . from which
everything in the universe comes, to which
everything in the universe returns . . . The natural
state of the universe unmanifest. Let go into the
clear light, trust it, merge with it. It is your own true
nature, it is home.

—*The Tibetan Book of the Dead*

It is solemn to remember that Vastness—
Is but the Shadow of the Brain which casts it—
All things swept sole away
This —is immensity—

—Emily Dickinson

To study Buddhism is to study ourselves. To study ourselves is to forget ourselves.

—Dōgen

Why run around sprinkling holy water?
There's an ocean inside you, and when you're ready you'll drink.

—Kabir

Having no destination, I am never lost.

—Ikkyū

. . . the individual is not a tool but a "vessel" of the divine.

—Max Weber, describing mysticism

204

The divine is not something high above us.
It is in heaven, it is in earth, it is inside us.

—Morihei Ueshiba

We sit together, the mountain and me,
until only the mountain remains.

—Li Po, "Zazen on Ching-t'ing Mountain"

The first peace . . . comes within the souls of
people when they . . . realize at the center of the
universe dwells the Great Spirit, and that its center
is really everywhere, it is within each of us.

—Black Elk

I don't think the mystical experience can be verbalized. When the ego disappears, so does power over language.

—W. H. Auden

Mysticism and exaggeration go together. A mystic must not fear ridicule if he is to push all the way to the limits of humility or the limits of delight.

—Milan Kundera

The world is like a Mask dancing. If you want to see it well, you do not stand in one place.

—Chinua Achebe

The Mystical

I celebrate myself, and sing myself,
And what I assume you shall assume,
For every atom belonging to me as good belongs
to you.

—Walt Whitman, "Song of Myself"

That is where my dearest and brightest dreams
have ranged—to hear for the duration of a heartbeat
the universe and the totality of life in its mysterious,
innate harmony.

—Herman Hesse

Human evolution has two steps—from being
somebody to being nobody; and from being nobody
to being everybody.

—Sri Sri Ravi Shankar

The Self is hidden in the hearts of all, as butter lies hidden in cream.
Realize the Self in the depths of meditation;
The Lord of Love, supreme reality, who is the goal of all knowledge.
This is the highest mystical teaching.

—*The Shveteshvatara Upanishad*

You are not your body; you are the eye.
…
A human being is an eye—the rest is just flesh and bones.
Whatever your eye sees, you are that.

—Rumi

The Mystical

At the sound of the bell
in the silent night,
I wake from my dream
in this dream world of ours.

Gazing at the reflection
of the moon in a clear pool,
I see, beyond my form, my real form.

—Kojisei

I'll tell you what: I believe mysticism is a very
serious endeavor. One must be equipped for it.

—Elie Wiesel

I once listened to an Indian on television say that God was in the wind and the water, and I wondered at how beautiful that was because it meant you could swim in Him or have Him brush your face in a breeze.

—Donald Miller

The soul should always stand ajar, ready to welcome the ecstatic experience.

—Emily Dickinson

If you're afraid of being grabbed by God, don't look at a wall. Definitely don't sit still.

—Jiyu Kennett

The Mystical

What does mysticism really mean? It means the way to attain knowledge. It's close to philosophy, except in philosophy you go horizontally while in mysticism you go vertically.

—Elie Wiesel

Once upon a time, I dreamt I was a butterfly . . . I was conscious only of my happiness as a butterfly, unaware that I was myself. Soon I awaked, and there I was, veritably myself again. Now I do not know whether I was then a man dreaming I was a butterfly, or whether I am now a butterfly, dreaming I am a man.

—Zhuangzi

The Tao that can be told is not the eternal Tao.
The name that can be named is not the eternal name.

—Lao Tzu, *Tao Te Ching*

211

If you want the secret of Buddhism, here it is:
Everything is in the Heart.

—Ryōkan

Zen does not confuse spirituality with thinking
about God while one is peeling potatoes. Zen
spirituality is just to peel the potatoes.

—Alan Wilson Watts

My miracle is that when I feel hungry I eat, and
when I feel thirsty I drink.

—Bankei Yōtaku, in response to a challenge to
demonstrate miraculous powers

The Mystical

I neither follow the Way nor depart from it. I neither
worship the Buddha nor have contempt for Him.
I neither sit long hours nor sit idle. I neither eat
one meal a day nor am I greedy for more. I desire
nothing and that is what I call the Way.

—Bassui Tokushō

You ask me why I dwell in the green mountain;
I smile and make no reply for my heart is free of
care.
As the peach-blossom flows down stream
and is gone into the unknown,
I have a world apart that is not among men.

—Li Po

The Mystical

The Holy Land is everywhere.

—Black Elk

I had been my whole life a bell and never knew it
until at that moment I was lifted and struck.

—Annie Dillard, describing a transcendental
experience with a tree

Mystics understand the roots of the Tao but not its
branches; scientists understand its branches but
not its roots.

—Fritjof Capra

To know what is impenetrable to us really exists,
manifesting itself as the highest wisdom and the
most radiant beauty, which our dull faculties can
comprehend only in their most primitive forms . . .
`this feeling is at the center of true religiousness.

—Albert Einstein

KYE HO! Wonderful!
You may say "existence," but you can't grasp it!
You may say "nonexistence," but many things
appear!
It is beyond the sky of "existence" and
"nonexistence"—
I know it but cannot point to it!

—Dakini Lion-Face

216

The Mystical

I hear and behold God in every object, yet
understand God not in the least . . .

                    —Walt Whitman, "Song of Myself"

The eye through which I see God is the same eye
through which God sees me; my eye and God's eye
are one eye, one seeing, one knowing, one love.

                    —Meister Eckhart

"What are we born for?"
"For infinite happiness," said the Spirit. "You can step out into it at any moment . . . "

—C. S. Lewis, *The Great Divorce*

This isn't instant coffee. There is no instant mysticism.

—Elie Wiesel

The Mystical

Of all that God has shown me
I can speak just the smallest word,
Not more than a honey bee
Takes on his foot
From an overspilling jar.

—Mechthild of Magdeburg

I am the life-force power of the universe. I am
the life-force power of the 50 trillion beautiful
molecular geniuses that make up my form, at one
with all that is.

—Jill Bolte Taylor

219

WHO has not found the heaven below
Will fail of it above.
God's residence is next to mine,
His furniture is love.

—Emily Dickinson

I cannot say
which is which:
the glowing
plum blossom is
the spring night's moon.

—Izumi Shikibu

The Mystical

To be alive, to be able to see, to walk, to have houses, music, paintings—it's all a miracle.

—Arthur Rubinstein

Just as in earthly life lovers long for the moment when they are able to…let their souls blend in a soft whisper, so the mystic longs for the moment when in prayer he can…creep into God.

—Søren Kierkegaard

Welcome the one who has kissed you from within. It is from inside everything comes.

—Mooji

This tremendous world I have inside of me. How to free myself, and this world, without tearing myself to pieces. And rather tear myself to a thousand pieces than be buried with this world within me.

—Franz Kafka

In the faith which is "God's marriage to the soul," you are one in God, and God is wholly in you...With this faith, in prayer you descend into yourself to meet the other.

—Dag Hammarskjöld

The Mystical

The coming of the kingdom of God is not
something that can be observed, nor will people
say, "Here it is," or "There it is," because the
kingdom of God is in your midst.

—*The Holy Bible*, Luke 17:21

For the enlightened, all that exists is nothing but
the Self,
So how could any suffering or delusion continue
for those who know this oneness?

—*The Isha Upanishad*

223

I looked for God. I went to a temple and I didn't find him there. Then I went to a church and I didn't find him there. The I went to a mosque and I didn't find him there. Then finally I looked in my heart and there he was.

—Rumi

All sentient beings are essentially Buddhas.

—Hakuin

The Mystical

In each individual the spirit has become flesh…

—Herman Hesse

We must become astronauts and go out into the universe and discover the God in ourselves.

—Ray Bradbury

I took a deep breath and listened to the old brag of my heart. I am, I am, I am.

—Sylvia Plath, *The Bell Jar*

In the dark night of the soul, bright flows the river of God.

—St. John of the Cross

Every man contemplates an angel in his future self.

—Ralph Waldo Emerson

Man is the supreme Talisman.

—Bahá'u'lláh

When a man has developed a high state of spirituality he can understand that the kingdom of heaven is within him.

— Swami Vivekananda

Jesus knew—knew—that we're carrying the Kingdom of Heaven around with us, inside, where we're all too goddam stupid and sentimental and unimaginative to look . . .

—J. D. Salinger, *Zooey*

I am aware of something in myself whose shine is my reason. I see clearly that something is there, but what it is I cannot understand. But it seems to me that, if I could grasp it, I should know all truth.

—Anonymous Christian mystic

There's this beautiful ocean of bliss and consciousness that is able to be reached by any human being by diving within.

—David Lynch

The Mystical

What? Whad'ya mean, "Where is he right now?"
In your consciousness! In your consciousness!
That where 'im always lived—in your
consciousness, ya dig it?

   —Bob Marley, responding to an interviewer's
    question on where God is right now

…what's heaven? what's earth? All in the mind.

      —Jack Kerouac

Only that day dawns to which we are awake.

      —Henry David Thoreau

Who looks outside, dreams; who looks inside,
awakens.

      —Carl Jung

REALIZING THE SELF

Live on, survive, for the earth gives forth wonders.
It may swallow your heart, but the wonders keep
on coming. You stand before them bareheaded,
shriven. What is expected of you is attention.

—Salmon Rushdie

The greatest discovery of my generation is that
man can alter his life simply by altering his attitude
of mind.

—James Trunslow Adams

Waking up this morning, I smile. Twenty-four brand new hours are before me. I vow to live fully in each moment and to look at all beings with eyes of compassion.

—Thích Nhất Hạnh

Knowing others is wisdom; knowing the self is enlightenment.

—Lao Tzu, *Tao Te Ching*

The spiritual path—is simply the journey of living our lives. Everyone is on a spiritual path; most people just don't know it.

—Marianne Williamson

Understanding the beauty of our humanity unlocks the power of our spirituality.

—Steve Maraboli

Man is lost and is wandering in a jungle where real values have no meaning. Real values can have meaning to man only when he steps on to the spiritual path, a path where negative emotions have no use.

—Sai Baba

Life no longer seemed like a series of Random events . . . I also began to see that being Rich and Famous wasn't going to bring me lasting fulfillment and that it was not the end of the journey.

—Madonna, on her Kabbalah faith

233

All spiritual journeys are martyrdoms.

—Jean Cocteau

One thing: you have to walk, and create the way by your walking; you will not find a ready-made path.

—Osho

The soul, like the body, lives by what it feeds on.

—J. G. Holland

It is the unseen and the spiritual in people that determines the outward and the actual.

—Oswald Chambers

[God] will use you to accomplish great things on the
condition that you believe much more in his love
than in your weakness.

—Mother Teresa

Lord, make me an instrument of thy peace.
Where there is hatred, let me sow love,
Where there is injury, pardon;
Where there is doubt, faith;
Where there is despair, hope;
Where there is darkness, light;
And where there is sadness, joy.

—St. Francis of Assisi

235

Should a person do good, let him do it again and again. Let him find pleasure therein, for blissful is the accumulation of good.

—The Buddha, *The Dhammapada*

Be joyful because it is humanly possible.

—Wendell Berry

Try to find pleasure in the speed that you're not used to. Changing the way you do routine things allows a new person to grow inside of you.

—Paulo Coelho

Realizing the Self

There are victories of the soul and spirit.
Sometimes, even if you lose, you win.

—Elie Wiesel

We do not believe in ourselves until someone
reveals that deep inside us something is valuable,
worth
listening to, worthy of our trust, sacred to our touch.

—E. E. Cummings

Some people, no matter how old they get, never
lose their beauty—they merely move it from their
faces into their hearts.

—Martin Buxbaum

Be conscious of God and speak always the truth.

—Barack Obama, quoting from *The Holy Quran*

To every man is given the key to the gates of heaven; the same key opens the gates of hell.

—Buddhist saying

Your own soul is nourished when you are kind, but you destroy yourself when you are cruel.

—*The Holy Bible*, Proverbs 11:17

To err is human; to forgive, divine.

—Alexander Pope

Realizing the Self

Words can sometimes, in moments of grace, attain the quality of deeds.

—Elie Wiesel

Neither fire nor wind, birth nor death can erase our good deeds.

—The Buddha

We must never stop dreaming. Dreams provide nourishment for the soul, just as a meal does for the body.

—Paulo Coelho, *The Pilgrimage*

Where is your water? Know your garden.

—Hopi teaching

When you do things from your soul you feel a river moving in you, a joy. When actions come from another section, the feeling disappears.

—Rumi

Be content with what you have; rejoice in the way things are. When you realize there is nothing lacking, the whole world belongs to you.

—Lao Tzu, *Tao Te Ching*

If anything is worth doing, do it with all your heart.

—The Buddha, *The Dhammapada*

Sincerity is the end and beginning of things;
without sincerity there would be nothing.

—Confucius

Certainly it is correct to say: Conscience is the voice
of God.

—Ludwig Wittgenstein

I am a red man. If the Great Spirit had desired me
to be a white man he would have made me so. . . .
Each man is good in his sight. It is not necessary
for Eagles to be Crows. We are poor . . . but we are
free.

—Sitting Bull

Where the soul is full of peace and joy,
outward surrounding and circumstances are of
comparatively little account.

—Hannah Whitall Smith

If, in our heart, we still cling to anything—anger,
anxiety, or possessions—we cannot be free.

—Thích Nhất Hạnh

If a man is to live, he must be all alive, body, soul,
mind, heart, spirit.

—Thomas Merton

To be a light to others you will need a good dose of the spiritual life. Because as my mother used to say, if you are in a good place, then you can help others; but if you're not well, then go look for somebody who is in a good place who can help you.

—Rigoberta Menchú

The soul is placed in the body like a rough diamond; and must be polished, or the lustre of it will never appear.

—Daniel Defoe

If you concentrate on finding whatever is good in every situation, you will discover that your life will suddenly be filled with gratitude.

—Rabbi Harold Kushner

244

Realizing the Self

Never despair . . .

—Horace

Our own life has to be our message.

—Thích Nhất Hạnh

'Be not afraid of life. Believe that life is worth living, and your belief will help create the fact.

—William James

Your life is your spiritual path. It's what's right in front of you. You can't live anyone else's life. The task is to live yours and stop trying to copy one you think looks better.

—Sandy Nathan

We've all got both light and dark inside us. What matters is the part we choose to act on. That's who we really are.

—J. K. Rowling, *Harry Potter and the Order of the Phoenix*

The path isn't a straight line; it's a spiral. You continually come back to things you thought you understood and see deeper truths.

—Barry H. Gillespie

If you don't know where you are going, any road will get you there.

—Lewis Carroll

246

Why do you so earnestly seek the truth in distant places?
Look for delusion and truth in the bottom of your own hearts.

—Ryōkan

Your breathing. The beating of your heart. The expansion of your lungs. Your mere presence is all that is needed to establish your worth.

—Iyanla Vanzant

You have to grow from the inside out. None can teach you, none can make you spiritual. There is no other teacher but your own soul.

—Swami Vivekananda

Never forget that you are not in the world; the world is in you. When anything happens to you, take the experience inward. Creation is set up to bring you constant hints and clues about your role as co-creator.

—Deepak Chopra

The soul is dyed the color of its thoughts. Think only on those things that are in line with your principles and can bear the light of day.

—Heraclitus

Truth is not a path you follow, but one created by your footsteps.

—Frederick E. Dodson

Realizing the Self

These days I am not bothering about
Getting enlightenment all the time,
And the result is that
I wake up in the morning feeling fine.

—Bankei Yōtaku

There is a road in the hearts of all of us, hidden and
seldom traveled, which leads to an unknown, secret
place.

—Luther Standing Bear

You cannot believe in God until you believe in
yourself.

—Swami Vivekananda

I think it's a mistake to ever look for hope outside of one's self.

—Arthur Miller, *After the Fall*

If we have not found heaven within, it is a certainty we will not find it without.

—Henry Miller

You and your purpose in life are the same thing. Your purpose is to be you.

—George Alexiou

Realizing the Self

If we would know what heaven is before we come thither, let us retire into the depths of our own spirits, and we shall find it there among holy thoughts and feelings.

—Nathaniel Hawthorne

Turn your face to the sun and the shadows fall behind you.

—Maori proverb

All human nature vigorously resists grace because grace changes us and the change is painful.

—Flannery O'Connor

251

Never place a period where God has placed a comma.

—Gracie Allen

I began to see that my problems, seen spiritually, were really my soul's plusses.

—Lionel Blue

The most exquisite paradox . . . as soon as you give it all up, you can have it all. As long as you want power, you can't have it. The minute you don't want power, you'll have more than you ever dreamed possible.

—Ram Dass

I had anger but never hate. Before the war, I was too busy studying to hate. After the war, I thought, What's the use? To hate would be to reduce myself.

—Elie Wiesel

When you recover or discover something that nourishes your soul and brings joy, care enough about yourself to make room for it in your life.

—Jean Shinoda Bolen

Everybody can be great. Because anybody can serve. You don't have to have a college degree to serve . . . You only need a heart full of grace. A soul generated by love.

—Martin Luther King, Jr.

253

Happiness cannot be traveled to, owned, earned, worn or consumed. Happiness is the spiritual experience of living every minute with love, grace, and gratitude.

—Denis Waitley

The possession of anything begins in the mind.

—Bruce Lee

The person who lives completely free from desires, without longing, devoid of the sense of "I" and "mine," attains peace.

—*The Bhagavad Gita*

Realizing the Self

God, grant me the serenity to accept the things I cannot change, the courage to change the things I can, and the wisdom to know the difference.

—Reinhold Niebuhr

It isn't until you come to a spiritual understanding of who you are—not necessarily a religious feeling, but deep down, the spirit within—that you can begin to take control.

—Oprah Winfrey

If you don't have a spiritual practice in place when times are good, you can't expect to suddenly develop one during a moment of crisis.

—Doug Coupland

255

Have courage for the great sorrows of life and patience for the small ones; and when you have laboriously accomplished your daily task, go to sleep in peace. God is awake.

—Victor Hugo

The essence of faith is fewness of words and abundance of deeds.

— Bahá'u'lláh

Every man is guilty of all the good he didn't do.

—Voltaire

To attain inner peace you must actually give your life, not just your possessions . . . then, and only then, can you begin to find inner peace.

—Peace Pilgrim

You can out-distance that which is running after you, but not what is running inside you.

—Rwandan proverb

He who knows that enough is enough will always have enough.

—Lao Tzu, *Tao Te Ching*

You may drink the ocean dry; you may uproot from its base the mountain Meru; you may swallow fire. But more diffucult than all these, oh Good One! is control over the mind.

—Yogi Ramacharaka

There's no value in digging shallow wells in a hundred places. Decide on one place and dig deep . . . If you leave that to dig another well, all the first effort is wasted and there is no proof you won't hit rock again.

—Swami Satchidananda

If you don't behave as you believe, you will end by believing as you behave.

—Fulton J. Sheen

The deeper you get into Yoga you realize it is a spiritual practice. It's a journey I'm making. I'm heading that way.

—Sting

Forgiveness is not an occasional act, it is a constant attitude.

—Martin Luther King, Jr.

Humility is not cowardice. Meekness is not weakness. Humility and meekness are indeed spiritual powers.

—Swami Sivānanda

Intuition is a spiritual faculty and does not explain, but simply points the way.

—Florence Scovel Shinn

If a man speaks or acts with a pure thought, happiness follows him, like a shadow that never leaves him.

—*The Dhammapada*, V. 1-2

Man cannot live without joy; therefore when he is deprived of true spiritual joys it is necessary that he become addicted to carnal pleasures.

—St. Thomas Aquinas

Realizing the Self

Life is a series of natural and spontaneous changes.
Don't resist them; that only creates sorrow. Let
reality be reality. Let things flow naturally forward in
whatever way they like.

—Lao Tzu, *Tao Te Ching*

Happiness is when what you think, what you say,
and what you do are in harmony.

—Mahatma Gandhi

The peace of God is with them whose mind and
soul are in harmony, who are free from desire and
wrath, who know their own soul.

—*The Bhagavad Gita*

261

If a man speaks or acts with an evil thought, pain follows him.
If a man speaks or acts with a pure thought, happiness follows him, like a shadow that never leaves him.

—The Buddha, *The Dhammapada*

You do not need to work to become spiritual. You are spiritual; you need only to remember that fact. Spirit is within you. God is within you.

—Julia Cameron

The things that we love tell us what we are.

—St. Thomas Aquinas

Always say "yes" to the present moment. What could be more futile, more insane, than to create inner resistance to what already is?

—Eckhart Tolle

Preach the Gospel at all times, and when necessary, use words.

—St. Francis of Assisi

Bring into play the almighty power within you, so that on the stage of life you can fulfill your high destined role.

—Paramahansa Yogananda

And as we let our own light shine, we unconsciously give other people permission to do the same.

—Marianne Williamson

Instead of trying to manipulate life to avoid
uncertainty, simply take an innocent attitude
instead. There are no guarantees here that things
will go right, there is only danger and mystery.
Courage means to be willing to go forward
nonetheless.

—Osho

In the end, it's not going to matter how many
breaths you took, but how many moments took
your breath away.

—Shing Xiong

All journeys have secret destinations of which the traveler is unaware.

—Martin Buber

I think a spiritual journey is not so much a journey of discovery. It's a journey of recovery. It's a journey of uncovering your own inner nature. It's already there.

—Billy Corgan

I think that I am a reflection, like the moon on water. When you see me, and I try to be a good man, you see yourself.

—The Dalai Lama, *Kundun*

HEALING THE WORLD

You can find Calcutta anywhere in the world. You only need two eyes to see. . . . There are people that are not loved, people that are not wanted nor desired, people that no one will help, people that are pushed away or forgotten. And this is the greatest poverty.

—Mother Teresa

It is wonderful how much time good people spend fighting the devil. If they would only expend the same amount of energy loving their fellow men, the devil would die in his own tracks of ennui.

—Helen Keller

If you keep your eyes so fixed on Heaven that you never look at the Earth, you will stumble into Hell.

—Austin O'Malley

The greatest religious problem today is how to be both a mystic and a militant; in other words how to combine the search for an expansion of inner awareness with effective social action.

—Ursula K. LeGuin

If we are to go forward, we must go back and rediscover those precious values—that all reality hinges on moral foundations and that all reality has spiritual control.

—Martin Luther King, Jr.

We're all going to die, all of us, what a circus! That alone should make us love each other. . . .

—Charles Bukowski, "The Captain is Out to Lunch
and the Sailors Have Taken Over the Ship"

The earth is but one country, and mankind its citizens.

—Bahá'u'lláh

We can find common ground only by moving to higher ground.

—Jim Wallis

The moment I have realized God sitting in the
temple of every human body, the moment I stand in
reverence before every human being and see God
in him . . . everything that binds vanishes, and
I am free.

—Swami Vivekananda

Only a philosophy of eternity, in the world today,
could justify non-violence.

—Albert Camus

Peace is a necessary condition of spirituality, no
less than an inevitable result of it.

—Aldous Huxley

Man has two great spiritual needs. One is for
forgiveness. The other is for goodness.

—Billy Graham

You must not lose faith in humanity. Humanity is
like an ocean; if a few drops of the ocean are dirty,
the ocean does not become dirty.

—Mahatma Gandhi

Hostilities aren't stilled through hostility, regardless.
Hostilities are stilled through non-hostility: this, an
unending truth.

—The Buddha, *The Dhammapada*

273

Healing the World

I feel the capacity to care is the thing which gives life its deepest significance.

—Pablo Casals

Our prime purpose in this life is to help others. And if you can't help them, at least don't hurt them.

—The Dalai Lama

An eye for an eye only ends up making the whole world blind.

—Mahatma Gandhi

True intimacy is the opening of one soul to another.

—Robert Sexton

Bread for myself is a material question. Bread for my neighbor is a spiritual one.

—Nikolai Berdyaev

I am not bothered by the fact that I am not understood. I am bothered when I do not know others.

—Confucius

Treat those who are good with goodness, and also treat those who are not good with goodness. Thus goodness is attained.

—Lao Tzu, *Tao Te Ching*

Healing the World

Compassion also brings us into the territory of mystery—encouraging us not just to see beauty, but perhaps also to look for the face of God in the moment of suffering, in the face of a stranger, in the face of the vibrant religious other.

—Krista Tippett

If you knew what I know about the power of giving, you would not let a single meal pass without sharing it in some way.

—The Buddha, *Itivuttika*

Hope is itself a species of happiness, and, perhaps, the chief happiness which this world affords.

—Samuel Johnson

277

Whoever destroys a soul, it is considered as if he destroyed an entire world. And whoever saves a life, it is considered as if he saved an entire world.

—*The Jerusalem Talmud,* Sanhedrin 4:1

My humanity is bound up in yours, for we can only be human together.

—Desmond Tutu

All human beings are also dream beings. Dreaming ties all mankind together.

—Jack Kerouac

A religious man is a person who holds God and man in one thought at one time, at all times, who suffers harm done to others, whose greatest passion is compassion, whose greatest strength is love and defiance of despair.

—Abraham Joshua Heschel

He said, stop asking God to bless what you're doing. Get involved in what God is doing—because it's already blessed.

—Bono, relating the story of a wise man's advice to him

The most terrifying fact about the universe is
not that it is hostile but that it is indifferent. . . .
However vast the darkness, we must supply our
own light.

—Stanley Kubrick

So I would hope they would develop some kind of
habit that involves understanding that their life is
so full they can afford to give in all kinds of ways
to other people. I consider that to be baseline
spirituality.

—Susan Sarandon

Healing the World

I have a great belief in spiritual force, but . . . that spiritual force alone has to have material force with it so long as we live in a material world. The two together make a strong combination.

—Eleanor Roosevelt

What is faith if it is not translated into action?

—Mahatma Gandhi

Religion is a way of walking, not a way of talking.

—William R. Inge

People seeking to live spiritually must be concerned with their social and physical environment.

—Sulak Sivaraksa

I was able to see faith as more than just a comfort to the weary or a hedge against death, but rather as an active, palpable agent in the world.

—Barack Obama

I don't think that God says, "Go to church and pray all day and everything will be fine." No. For me God says, "Go out and make the changes that need to be made, and I'll be there to help you."

—Elvia Alvarado

Sometimes I enter prayer and I intend to prolong it, but then I hear a child crying, and I shorten my prayer thinking of the distress of the child's mother.

—The Prophet Muhammad

Healing the World

The opposite of love is not hate, it's indifference.
The opposite of beauty is not ugliness, it's
indifference. The opposite of faith is not heresy, it's
indifference. And the opposite of life is not death,
but indifference between life and death.

—Elie Wiesel

You and I are created for transcendence, laughter,
caring. God deliberately did not make the world
perfect, for God is looking for you and me to be
fellow workers with God.

—Desmond Tutu

In our era, the road to holiness necessarily passes
through the world of action.

—Dag Hammarskjöld

I believe much trouble and blood would be saved if we opened our hearts more.

—Chief Joseph

There is a God and He is good, and His love, while free, has a self imposed cost: We must be good to one another.

—George H. W. Bush

God has always given me the strength to say what is right.

—Rosa Parks

For me, we all need to be Jesus in our time. Jesus' message was to love your neighbor as yourself and these are people in need.

—Madonna

Kindness is the touch of heaven, a reminder of the covenant of the unseen.

—Mark Anthony

Neither genius, fame, nor love show the greatness of the soul. Only kindness can do that.

—Henri-Dominique Lacordaire

The most powerful weapon on earth is the human soul on fire.

—Ferdinand Foch

If a man be gracious and courteous to strangers, it shows he is a citizen of the world, and that his heart is no island cut off from other lands, but a continent that joins them.

—Francis Bacon

All things are bound together, all things connect. Whatever befalls the earth, befalls also the children of the earth.

—Chief Oren Lyons

Healing the World

It is people's hearts that move the age.

—Herbie Hancock

How wonderful it is that nobody need wait a single moment before starting to improve the world.

—Anne Frank

Kindness holds the key to the secret of our own transformation and, in the process, of the transformation of the world.

—Jean Maalouf

Loving kindness is greater than laws; and the charities of life are more than all ceremonies.

—*The Talmud*

287

Kindness begets kindness evermore.

—Sophocles

A life of kindness is the primary meaning of divine worship.

—Emanuel Swedenborg

Be kind whenever possible. It is always possible.

—The Dalai Lama

There is no way to peace, peace is the way.

—A. J. Muste

If we have no peace, it is because we have forgotten that we belong to each other.

—Mother Teresa

Nonviolence is the first article of my faith. It is also the last article of my creed.

—Mahatma Gandhi

It isn't enough to talk about peace. One must believe in it. And it isn't enough to believe in it. One must work at it.

—Eleanor Roosevelt

Human Beings, indeed all sentient beings, have the right to pursue happiness and live in peace and freedom.

—The Dalai Lama

The pursuit of peace and progress, with its trials and its errors, its successes and its setbacks, can never be relaxed and never abandoned.

—Dag Hammarskjöld

To see the other side, to defend another people, not despite your tradition but because of it, is the heart of pluralism.

—Eboo Patel

Whether we are Christians or Muslims or
nationalists or agnostics or atheists, we must first
learn to forget our differences.

—Malcolm X

We may have different religions, different languages,
different colored skin, but we all belong to one
human race. We all share the same basic values.

—Kofi Annan

You're alive. That means you have infinite potential.
You can do anything, make anything, dream anything.
If you change the world, the world will change.

—Neil Gaiman, *The Graveyard Book*

291

They can't chain my spirit! My spirit runs free! Walls can't contain it! Laws can't restrain it! Authority has no power over it!

—Bill Watterson

Who knows, my God, but that the universe is not one vast sea of compassion actually, the veritable holy honey, beneath all this show of personality and cruelty?

—Jack Kerouac

Healing the World

The earth does not belong to man, man belongs to
the earth. All things are connected like the blood
that unites us all. Man did not weave the web of
life, he is merely a strand in it. Whatever he does to
the web, he does to himself.

—Chief Seattle

People in ignorance say, "My religion is the only
one, my religion is the best." But when a heart is
illumined by true knowledge, it knows that above all
these wars of sects...presides the one indivisible,
eternal, all-knowing bliss.

—Sri Ramakrishna

The Superior Man is all-embracing and not partial.
The inferior man is partial and not all-embracing.

—Confucius

293

All men are by nature equal, all made of the same earth by one Workman; and however we may deceive ourselves, as dear unto God is the poor peasant as the mighty prince.

—Plato

Hindus, in their capacity for love, are indeed hairless Christians, just as Muslims, in the way they see God in everything, are bearded Hindus, and Christians, in their devotion to God, are hat-wearing Muslims.

—Yann Martel, *Life of Pi*

We who have been born Buddhist, Hindu, Christian, Muslim, or any other faith can be very comfortable in each others temple's, mosques, and churches, praying or meditating together to create a spiritual mass of consciousness which can overcome our greed, hatred, and illusions.

—Ari Ariyaratne

Show me a religion that doesn't care about compassion. Show me a religion that doesn't care about stewardship of the environment. Show me a religion that doesn't care about hospitality.

—Eboo Patel

295

The basis of world peace is the teaching which runs through almost all the great religions of the world. "Love thy neighbor as thyself."

—Eleanor Roosevelt

It is not our purpose to become each other; it is to recognize each other, to learn to see the other and honor him for what he is.

—Herman Hesse

God has given us many faiths but only one world in
which to co-exist. May your work help all of us to
cherish our commonalities and feel enlarged by our
differences.

—Jonathan Sacks

God is diverse and inclusive, not limited and
exclusive. You're thinking of a Country Club.

—Brian Robertson

297

If a person's religious ideas correspond not with your own, love him nevertheless. How different would yours have been, had the chance of birth placed you in Tartary or India!

—Percy Bysshe Shelley

All religions are branches of one big tree.

—George Harrison

The "sigh within the prayer is the same in the heart of the Christian, the Muslim, and the Jew." I have seen this unity with my eyes, heard it with my ears, felt it with all my being.

—David James Duncan

So we can only pray, if we are Hindus, not that
a Christian should become a Hindu . . . but our
innermost prayer should be a Hindu should be a
better Hindu, a Muslim a better Muslim, a Christian
a better Christian.

—Mahatma Gandhi

One of the most spiritual things you can do is
embrace your humanity. Connect with those around
you today. Say "I love you," "I'm sorry," "I appreciate
you," "I'm proud of you" . . . give plenty of hugs.

—Steve Maraboli

299

When I breathe in, I am breathing in the laughter, tears, victories, passions, thoughts, memories, existence, joys, moments, and the hues of the sunlight on many tones of skin; I am breathing in the same air that was exhaled by many before me . . . how can I ever say that I am alone?

—C. Joybell C.

I offer you peace. I offer you love. I offer you friendship. I see your beauty. I hear your need. I feel your feelings. My wisdom flows from the Highest Source. I salute that Source in you. Let us work together for unity and love.

—Mahatma Gandhi

Healing the World

I love you when you bow in your mosque, kneel in your temple, pray in your church. For you and I are sons of one religion, and it is the spirit.

—Khalil Gibran

We do not inherit the Earth from our Ancestors, we borrow it from our Children.

—Native American wisdom

We intend to make this world the most beautiful, glorious planet that any human being can imagine and, really, beyond anything any human being can imagine.

—Hafsat Abiola

I believe that man will not merely endure; he will prevail. He is immortal, not because he alone among the creatures has an inexhaustible voice, but because he has a soul, a spirit capable of kindness and compassion.

—William Faulkner, in his Nobel Prize acceptance speech

When I despair, I remember that all through history the ways of truth and love have always won. There have been tyrants, and murderers, and for a time they can seem invincible, but in the end they always fall. Think of it—always.

—Mahatma Gandhi

fr. Gr. limber; supple.]
Gr. *lithos* stone.]

fr. Gr. *lithos* stone;
Chem. A so...
the lightest me...
wt., 6.94.
prefix meaning...
otomy.
[litho- + -graph...
by lithograb...
hy. **li·thog'ra·ph...**
[litho- + -graph...
riting of designs...
with a greasy...
impression fr...
[Gk.] *adj.*
are sphere.]
pare Armour...

Ll. fr. Gr...
urgical rev...

t can be treated.

law. — To...
al process...
I. *jurisp...*
involved in, d...

Richard...
A 'li...
tapped rod t...
swell.

irish flannel...

LOVE

When you plant a seed of love, it is you that blossoms.

—Ma Jaya

Like when you sit in front of a fire in winter—you are just there in front of the fire. You don't have to be smart or anything. The fire warms you.

—Desmond Tutu

The most telling and profound way of describing the evolution of the universe would undoubtedly be to trace the evolution of love.

—Pierre Teilhard de Chardin

Beyond all reason is the mystery of love.

—Robin Craig Clark

"What is hell?" I maintain that it is the suffering of being unable to love.

—Fyodor Dostoevsky, *The Brothers Karamazov*

And though I have the gift of prophecy, and understand all mysteries, and all knowledge; and though I have all faith, so that I could remove mountains, but have not love, I am nothing.

—*The Holy Bible,* 1 Corinthians 13:2

Love

God is love; so God is beyond the law, for love is above the law.

—Hazrat Inayat Khan

Love in its essence is spiritual fire.

—Lucius Annaeus Seneca

When two people relate to each other authentically and humanly, God is the electricity that surges between them.

—Martin Buber

[Love] is perhaps the only glimpse we are permitted of eternity.

—Helen Hayes

307

Love is holy because it is like grace—the worthiness of its object is never really what matters.

—Marilynne Robinson, *Gilead*

The door you open to give love is the very one through which love arrives.

—Alan Cohen

Your task is not to seek for love, but merely to seek and find all the barriers within yourself that you have built against it.

—Rumi

Love

Immature love says, "I love you because I need you."
Mature love says, "I need you because I love you."

—Erich Fromm

Being deeply loved by someone gives you strength,
while loving someone deeply gives you courage.

—Lao Tzu, *Tao Te Ching*

Love is not an emotion. It is your very existence.

—Sri Sri Ravi Shankar

Oh, love isn't there to make us happy. I believe it
exists to show us how much we can endure.

—Herman Hesse

309

If we don't love ourselves, we would not love others.

—Supreme Master Ching Hai

Thus is the nature of love: that you must use it! A love unused is not love! If it is something that sits on the shelf that you don't know what to do with, it is not true to the nature of love! Use love!

—C. Joybell C.

To say that I am made in the image of God is to say that Love is the reason for my existence . . . Love is my true identity . . . Love is my true character. Love is my name.

—Thomas Merton

Love

Love all God's creation, both the whole and every
grain of sand. Love every leaf, every ray of light . . .
If you love each thing you will perceive the mystery
of God in all.

—Fyodor Dostoevsky

Love is what we were born with. Fear is what
we learned here. The spiritual journey is the
relinquishment, or unlearning, of fear and the
acceptance of love back into our hearts.

—Marianne Williamson

If only you could love enough, you could be the
happiest and most powerful being in the world.

—Emmet Fox

In a day, sometimes I feel so much love for the world, I think my heart is bursting. Sometimes, I feel so scared, I want to shrink myself even further. I think that's what happened to us gods and goddesses.

—Yoko Ono

The soul is not where it lives, but where it loves.

—Anonymous

God's love for us is not the reason for which we should love him. God's love for us is the reason for us to love ourselves.

—Simone Weil

Love

Legalism says God will love us if we change. The
gospel says God will change us because He loves us.

—Tullian Tchividjian

Love is the emblem of eternity; it confounds all
notion of time; effaces all memory of a beginning,
all fear of an end . . .

—Germaine de Staël

Love is a sacred reserve of energy; it is like the
blood of spiritual evolution.

—Pierre Teilhard de Chardin

And now these three remain: faith, hope and love. But the greatest of these is love.

—*The Holy Bible*, 1 Corinthians 13:13

The soul is made of love and must ever strive to return to love. . . . It must lose itself in love. By its very nature it must seek God, who is love.

—Mechthild of Magdenburg

Dear friends, let us love one another, for love comes from God. Everyone who loves has been born of God and knows God. Whoever does not love does not know God, because God is love.

—*The Holy Bible,* 1 John 4:7-8

Love

The kind of love that God has for us . . . is of an
infinite longing for union, and the kind of love that
God wants us to have for him . . . is of this also
endless longing.

—Kevin Hart

Divine love is a sacred flower, which in its early bud
is happiness, and in its full bloom is heaven.

—Eleanor Brown

Darkness cannot drive out darkness; only light can
do that. Hate cannot drive out hate; only love can
do that.

—Martin Luther King, Jr.

Joy is prayer—Joy is strength—Joy is love—Joy is a net of love by which you can catch souls.

—Mother Teresa

[Love] comes out of heaven, unasked and unsought.

—Pearl S. Buck

To love someone means to see him as God intended him.

—Fyodor Dostoevsky

Love

Work without love is slavery.

—Mother Teresa

He who has love for other people has God in his
heart. To serve God's children is to serve God.

—Supreme Master Ching Hai

LOVE is anterior to life,
Posterior to death,
Initial of creation, and
The exponent of breath.

—Emily Dickinson

Love is an act of faith, and whoever is of little faith is also of little love.

—Erich Fromm

When angels speak of love they tell us it is only by loving that we enter an earthly paradise. They tell us paradise is our home and love our true destiny.

—bell hooks

Love

This is what our love is—a sacred pattern of unbroken unity sewn flawlessly invisible inside all other images, thoughts, smells, and sounds.

—Aberjhani

The first question which the priest and the Levite asked was: "If I stop to help this man, what will happen to me?" But . . . the good Samaritan reversed the question: "If I do not stop to help this man, what will happen to him?"

—Martin Luther King, Jr.

Where there is love there is life.

—Mahatma Gandhi

Be drunk in love, since love is everything that exists.

—Rumi

What if sometimes there is no choice about what to love? What if the temple comes to Mohammed? What if you just love? without deciding?

—David Foster Wallace, *Infinite Jest*

. . . there is nothing that we can do but love . . .

—Dorothy Day

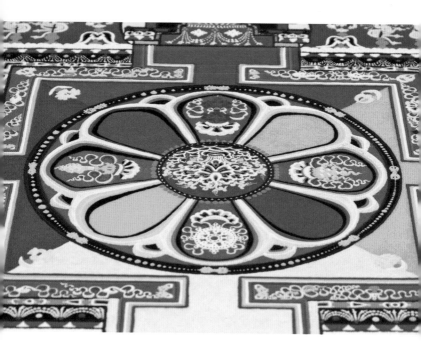

ART

The goal of life is rapture. Art is the way we experience it. Art is the transforming experience.

—Joseph Campbell

To send light into the darkness of men's hearts— such is the duty of the artist.

—Robert Schumann

Art is my spiritual path. . . . Art is my prayer, my ritual, my remembrance of the Divine. Art is the way I knit together the beliefs and practices that guide my life.

—Pat B. Allen

Art is the stored honey of the human soul, gathered on wings of misery and travail.

—Theodore Dreiser

[Faith] is the key that negates the impossible. To deny faith is to refute . . . the spirit that generates all our creative forces.

—Charlie Chaplin

I never liked jazz music because jazz music doesn't resolve. But I was outside the Bagdad Theater in Portland one night when I saw a man playing the saxophone . . . After that I liked jazz music. I used to not like God because God didn't resolve. But that was before any of this happened.

—Donald Miller

Art

By art alone we are able to get outside ourselves,
to know what another sees of this universe which
for him is not ours . . .

—Marcel Proust, *Remembrance of Things Past*

The world speaks to me in colours, my soul
answers in music.

—Rabindranath Tagore

When I have a terrible need of—shall I say the
word—religion. Then I go out and paint the stars.

—Vincent Van Gogh

Art is Man's nature. Nature is God's art.

—Philip James Bailey

Art is a collaboration between God and the artist,
and the less the artist does the better.

— André Gide

I've always been spiritual . . . and it took me a while
to find the proper context. It's hard to realize you can
have any kind of relationship with God you want . . .
and so I now have a punk rock relationship with God.

—Billy Corgan

You use a glass mirror to see your face: you use
works of art to see your soul.

—George Bernard Shaw

What art offers is space—a certain breathing room
for the spirit.

—John Updike

Where the spirit does not work with the hand there is no art.

—Leonardo Da Vinci

The true work of art is but a shadow of the divine perfection.

—Michelangelo

Art is spirituality in drag.

—Jennifer Yane

For the mystic what is how. For the craftsman how is what. For the artist what and how are one.

—William McElcheran

328

Art

Art has two constant, two unending concerns: It always meditates on death and thus always creates life. All great, genuine art resembles and continues the Revelation of St John.

—Boris Pasternak

I think creativity is spiritual. I absolutely believe that.

—F. Murray Abraham

We are ourselves creations. We are meant to continue creativity by being creative ourselves. This is the God-force extending itself through us.

—Julia Cameron

My imagination flows through God's eyes.

—Nick Vujicic

Imagination is the voice of daring. If there is anything Godlike about God it is that. He dared to imagine everything.

—Henry Miller, *Tropic of Capricorn*

Art

We do not need magic to change the world, we
carry all the power we need inside ourselves
already: we have the power to imagine better.

—J. K. Rowling

Imagination is the eye of the soul.

—Joseph Joubert

Fantasy remains a human right: we make in our
measure and in our derivative mode, because we
are made: and not only made, but made in the
image and likeness of a Maker.

—J. R. R. Tolkien

Reason is the natural order of truth; but imagination is the organ of meaning.

—C. S. Lewis

Imagination is the vehicle through which faith is expressed.

—Cheryl Forbes

All our other faculties seem to have the brown touch of earth upon them, but the imagination carries the very livery of heaven, and is God's self in the soul.

—Henry Ward Beecher

Art

Without Art, we should have no notion of the sacred; without Science, we should always worship false gods.

—W. H. Auden

We're creators by permission, by grace as it were. . . . An artist is an instrument that registers something already existent, something which belongs to the whole world, and which, if he is an artist, he is compelled to give back to the world.

—Henry Miller

A painting is not about an experience. It is an experience.

—Mark Rothko

Art is not made to decorate rooms. It is an offensive weapon in the defense against the enemy.

—Pablo Picasso

Paintings have a life of their own that derives from the painter's soul.

—Vincent Van Gogh

Painting isn't an aesthetic operation; it's a form of magic designed as mediator between this strange hostile world and us.

—Pablo Picasso

Music is the mediator between the spiritual and the sensual life.

—Ludwig van Beethoven

Art

Those who sing pray twice.

—St. Augustine of Hippo

Music is my life and my life is music. Anyone who does not understand this is not worthy of God.

—Wolfgang Amadeus Mozart

If I should ever die, God forbid, let this be my epitaph:

THE ONLY PROOF HE NEEDED
FOR THE EXISTENCE OF GOD
WAS MUSIC

—Kurt Vonnegut

Music is the one incorporeal entrance into the higher world of knowledge which comprehends mankind but which mankind cannot comprehend.

—Ludwig van Beethoven

The music that really turns me on is either running toward God or away from God. Both recognize the pivot, that God is at the center of the jaunt.

—Bono

Hip-Hop isn't just music, it is also a spiritual movement of the blacks! You can't just call Hip-Hop a trend!

—Lauryn Hill

Art

My job in this life is to give people spiritual ecstasy
through music. In my concerts people cry, laugh,
dance. If they climaxed spiritually, I did my job.

—Carlos Santana

Music can also be a sensual pleasure, like eating
food or sex. But its highest vibration for me is
that point of taking us to a real understanding of
something in our nature which we can very rarely
get at. It is a spiritual state of oneness.

—Terry Riley

337

There is a kind of mysticism to writing.

—Irvine Welsh

A book, too, can be a star, a living fire to lighten the darkness, leading out into the expanding universe.

—Madeleine L'Engle

Although only breath, words which I command are immortal.

—Sappho

Art

I think we ought to read only the kind of books that wound or stab us. If the book we're reading doesn't wake us up with a blow to the head, what are we reading for? . . . A book must be the axe for the frozen sea within us. That is my belief.

—Franz Kafka

Words are also seeds, and when dropped into the invisible spiritual substance, they grow and bring forth after their kind.

—Charles Fillmore

We read to know that we are not alone.

—C. S. Lewis

A good book is an education of the heart. It enlarges your sense of human possibility what human nature is of what happens in the world. It's a creator of inwardness.

—Susan Sontag

We don't need a list of rights and wrongs, tables of dos and don'ts: we need books, time, and silence. Thou shalt not is soon forgotten, but Once upon a time lasts forever.

—Philip Pullman

I have always imagined that Paradise will be a kind of library.

—Jorge Luis Borges

340

When the Day of Judgment dawns and people
. . . come marching in to receive their heavenly
rewards, the Almighty will gaze upon the mere
bookworms and say to Peter, "Look, these need no
reward. We have nothing to give them. They have
loved reading."

—Virginia Woolf

LAUGHTER AND TEARS

A priest once quoted to me the Roman saying that
a religion is dead when the priests laugh at each
other across the altar. I always laugh at the altar, be
it Christian, Hindu, or Buddhist, because real religion
is the transformation of anxiety into laughter.

—Alan Wilson Watts

When anybody laughs, he has no mind, no thought,
no problem, no suffering.

—Sri H. W. L. Poonja

Laughter is the closest thing to the grace of God.

—Karl Bath

Humor is the contemplation of the finite from the point of view of the infinite.

—Christian Morgenstern

God is a comedian, playing to an audience too afraid to laugh.

—Voltaire

Seven days without laughter makes one weak.

—Mort Walker

He who laughs, lasts.

—Mary P. Poole

As God contains all good things, He must also contain a sense of playfulness—a gift he has shared with Creatures other than ourselves, as witness the tricks Crows play, and the sportiveness of Squirrels, and the frolicking of Kittens.

—Margaret Atwood, *The Year of the Flood*

Coincidences are spiritual puns.

—G. K. Chesterton

Eternity is a mere moment, just long enough for a joke.

—Herman Hesse

It is not funny that anything else should fall down, only that a man should fall down…Why do we laugh? Because it is a gravely religious matter: it is the Fall of Man. Only man can be absurd: for only man can be dignified.

—G. K. Chesterton, "Spiritualism"

God writes a lot of comedy . . . the trouble is, he's stuck with so many bad actors who don't know how to play funny.

—Garrison Keillor

A God who cannot smile could not have created
this humorous universe.

—Sri Aurobindo

. . . A Zen monk once said to me, "If you're not
laughing, then you're not getting it."

—David O. Russell

The greater your capacity to love, the greater your
capacity to feel the pain.

—Jennifer Aniston

It is amazing that our souls—our eternal essences, with all their hopes and dreams and visions of an eternal world—are contained within these temporal bodies. No wonder suffering is part of the human condition.

—Marion Woodman

Grief is the price we pay for love.

—Queen Elizabeth II

Crying is one of the highest devotional songs. One who knows crying, knows spiritual practice. If you can cry with a pure heart, nothing else compares to such a prayer.

—Kripalvanandji

Pain is inevitable. Suffering is optional.

— Buddhist proverb

Our comforts come from God; our sorrows, from ourselves.

—Ivan Panin

Remember that not getting what you want is sometimes a wonderful stroke of luck.

—The Dalai Lama

"Dear little Swallow," said the Prince, "you tell me of marvelous things, but more marvelous than anything is the suffering of men and of women. There is no Mystery so great as Misery."

—Oscar Wilde, *The Happy Prince and Other Tales*

There is no sun without shadow, and it is essential to know the night.

—Albert Camus

Who would ever know the greater graces of comfort and perseverance, mercy and forgiveness, patience and courage, if no shadows fell over a life?

—Ann Voskamp

Laughter and Tears

When people say they hate life, to what are they comparing it to? The alternative isn't any more appealing.

—Carroll Bryant

Man is born broken. He lives by mending. The grace of God is glue.

—Eugene O'Neill

Do not be afraid; our fate
Cannot be taken from us; it is a gift.

—Dante Alighieri, *Inferno*

Hell is not punishment. It's training.

—Shunryu Suzuki

Sorrow and silence are strong, and patient
endurance is godlike.

—Henry Wadsworth Longfellow

People have a hard time letting go of their suffering.
Out of a fear of the unknown, they prefer suffering
that is familiar.

—Thích Nhất Hạnh

The root of suffering is attachment.

—The Buddha

You don't really know Jesus is all you need until
Jesus is all you have.

—Timothy Keller

Laughter and Tears

Extreme hopes are born of extreme misery.

—Bertrand Russell

The miserable have no other medicine
But only hope.

—William Shakespeare, *Measure for Measure*

If it were not for pain, life would be most
uninteresting, for it is by pain that the heart is
penetrated.

—Hazrat Inayat Khan

There's a crack (or cracks) in everyone . . . that's
how the light of God gets in.

—Elizabeth Gilbert, *Eat, Pray, Love*

355

Earth has no sorrow that Heaven cannot heal.

—Thomas Moore

Ah done been in sorrow's kitchen and Ah done licked out all de pots. Ah done died in grief and been buried in de bitter waters, and Ah done rose agin from de dead lak Lazarus.

—Zora Neale Hurston, *Jonah's Gourd Vine*

In sorrow and in suffering are hidden the springs of a peace and a power that can be affected by no outward storms.

—Edwin Hubbell Chapin

Laughter and Tears

The soul would have no rainbow if the eyes had no tears.

—John Vance Cheney

You pray for rain, you gotta deal with the mud too. That's a part of it.

—Denzel Washington

They have never known pain, he thought. The realization made him feel desperately lonely.

—Lois Lowry, *The Giver*

The pleasure that is in sorrow is sweeter than the pleasure of pleasure itself.

—Percy Bysshe Shelley

Joy and sorrow are like milk and cookies. That's how well they go together.

—Neil Gaiman, *American Gods*

Jesus wept.

—*The Holy Bible*, John 11:35, when Jesus learns of Lazarus' death

Look at Jesus. He was perfect, right? And yet he goes around crying all the time. He is always weeping, a man of sorrows. Do you know why? Because he is perfect. Because when you are not all absorbed in yourself, you can feel the sadness of the world.

—Timothy Keller

Laughter and Tears

One drop of sorrow heals the troubled heart
More than a thousand tongues of consolation.

—Robert Leighton, "At the Grave of Margaret"

The excursion is the same when you go looking for
your sorrow as when you go looking for your joy.

—Eudora Welty, "The Wide Net"

Sorrow is how we learn to love. Your heart isn't
breaking. It hurts because it's getting larger. The
larger it gets, the more love it holds.

—Rita Mae Brown, *Riding Shotgun*

Let me not pray to be sheltered from dangers but
to be fearless in facing them.
Let me not beg for the stilling of my pain but for the
heart to conquer it.

—Rabindranath Tagore

What is to give light must endure burning.

—Viktor Frankl

Life is the soul's nursery—its training place for the
destinies of eternity.

—William Makepeace Thackeray

AFTERLIFE

Life is but a prelude.

—Edward Counsel

To the well-organized mind, death is but the next
great adventure.

—J. K. Rowling, *Harry Potter and the
Philosopher's Stone*

What deity in the realms of dementia, what
rabid god decocted out of the smoking lobes of
hydrophobia could have devised a keeping place
for souls so poor as is this flesh. This mawky
wormbent tabernacle.

—Cormac McCarthy, *Suttree*

Death is the protector of life and life is the process
of death.

—Wasif Ali Wasif

Life is like walking through Paradise with peas in
your shoes.

—Charles Edward Jerningham

Afterlife

The cradle rocks above an abyss, and common sense tells us that our existence is but a brief crack of light between two eternities of darkness.

—Vladimir Nabokov, *Speak, Memory*

The reason death sticks so closely to life isn't biological necessity—it's envy. Life is so beautiful that death has fallen in love with it, a jealous, possessive love that grabs at what it can.

—Yann Martel, *Life of Pi*

There is no birth, there is no death; there is no coming, there is no going; there is no same, there is no different; there is no permanent self, there is no annihilation. We only think there is.

—Thích Nhất Hạnh

365

How sweet! You still believe in death . . . that's just so . . . quaint. Well, sorry to pop your death bubble, but there's no such thing. So make the best of things. Any real belief in death is just wishful thinking.

—Chuck Palahniuk

No man has learned anything rightly, until he knows that every day is Doomsday.

—Ralph Waldo Emerson

. . . death is a highly creative force. The highest spiritual values of life can originate from the thought and study of death.

—Elisabeth Kubler-Ross

Afterlife

If you want immortality, then deny form. Whatever has form has mortality. Beyond form is the formless, the immortal.

—Frank Herbert, *God Emperor of Dune*

Do not seek death. Death will find you. But seek the road which makes death a fulfillment.

—Dag Hammarskjöld

Everything is passing . . . enjoy its momentariness.

—Mooji

Some do not understand that we must die, but those who do realize this settle their quarrels.

—The Buddha, *The Dhammapada*

Death is no more than passing from one room into another. But there's a difference for me, you know. Because in that other room I shall be able to see.

—Helen Keller

Maybe that's what life is . . . a wink of the eye and winking stars.

—Jack Kerouac

The reason we think of death in celestial terms is that the visible firmament, especially at night . . . is the most adequate and ever-present symbol of that vast silent explosion.

—Vladimir Nabokov, "That in Aleppo Once . . . "

Afterlife

I don't think I've found God, but I may have seen
where gods come from.

—Terry Pratchett, after contracting
Alzheimer's disease

Life is not a series of gig lamps symmetrically
arranged; life is a luminous halo, a semi-transparent
envelope surrounding us from the beginning of
consciousness to the end.

—Virginia Woolf, "Modern Fiction"

To be running breathlessly, but not yet arrived,
is itself delightful, a suspended moment of
living hope.

—Anne Carson

369

What is life? It is the flash of a firefly in the night. It is the breath of a buffalo in the wintertime. It is the little shadow which runs across the grass and loses itself in the sunset.

—Crowfoot

To die will be an awfully big adventure.

—J. M. Barrie, *Peter Pan*

When you were born, you cried, and the world rejoiced. Live your life in such a manner that when you die, the world cries and you rejoice.

—Cherokee proverb

Afterlife

One short sleep past, we wake eternally,
And death shall be no more; Death, thou shalt die.

—John Donne, *Holy Sonnets* "No. 10"

I hope it is true that a man can die and yet not
only live in others but give them . . . that great
consciousness of life.

—Jack Kerouac

They are not dead who live in the hearts they leave
behind.

—Tuscarora proverb

Your lost friends are not dead, but gone before,
advanced a stage or two upon that road which you
must travel in the steps they trod.

—Aristophanes

If your friend is sick and dying, the most important
thing he wants is not an explanation; he wants you
to sit with him. He's terrified of being alone more
than anything else. So, God has not left us alone.

—Lee Strobel

We should think of [death] as some sort of mystery
which we can participate in now, not something to
be pushed off to one side till the last moments.

—Kevin Hart

Afterlife

As death...is the true goal of our existence, I have formed during the last few years such close relationships with this best and truest friend of mankind that death's image is not only no longer terrifying to me, but is indeed very soothing and consoling.

—Wolfgang Amadeus Mozart

Has this world been so kind to you that you should leave with regret? There are better things ahead than any we leave behind.

—C. S. Lewis

[C.S.] Lewis radiated a sense that the spiritual world is home, that we are always coming back to a place we have never yet reached.

—David C. Downing

Love is God, and to die means that I, a particle of love, shall return to the general and eternal source.

—Leo Tolstoy, *War and Peace*

My soul is from elsewhere, I'm sure of that, and I intend to end up there.

—Rumi

We feel and experience ourselves to be eternal.

—Baruch Spinoza

Afterlife

Our hope of immortality does not come from any religions, but all religions come from that hope.

—Robert G. Ingersoll

One certainly has a soul; but how it came to allow itself to be enclosed in a body is more than I can imagine. I only know if once mine gets out, I'll have a bit of a tussle before I let it get in again to that of any other.

—Lord Byron

Life is what you celebrate. All of it. Even its end.

—Joanne Harris, *Chocolat*

It is the acceptance of death that has finally allowed
me to choose life.

—Elizabeth Lesser

What the caterpillar calls the end of the world, the
master calls a butterfly.

—Richard Bach

To me a heaven would be a big bull ring with
me holding two barrera seats and a trout stream
outside that no one else was allowed to fish in . . .

—Ernest Hemingway, in a letter to
F. Scott Fitzgerald

Afterlife

It is not death that a man should fear, but he should
fear never beginning to live.

—Marcus Aurelius

Death is the end of one story and the beginning of
another.

—Philip Moeller, Helena's Husband

Life is like a voyage that is homeward bound.

—Herman Melville

Every day is a journey, and the journey
itself is home.

—Basho

Why fear death? It is the most beautiful
adventure in life.

—Charles Frohman, his last words before drowning
in the RMS *Lusitania*

The call of death is a call of love. Death can be
sweet if we answer it in the affirmative, if we
accept it as one of the great eternal forms of life
and transformation.

—Hermann Hesse

Now at last they were beginning Chapter One of
the Great Story no one on earth has ever read:
which goes on forever: in which every chapter is
better than the one before.

—C. S. Lewis, *The Last Battle*

Afterlife

That's the happiest moment. When it's all done.
When we stop. When we can stop.

—Edward Albee, *Three Tall Women*

There will come a time when you believe everything
is finished. That will be the beginning.

—Louis L'Amour

INDEX

Index

383

Index

Index

Index

Index

Index